D0349601

HIGHLAND
LIB

WITH

PAUL MARTIN
My World of Antiques

*This book is dedicated
to my two children,
Dylan and Meredith*

PAUL MARTIN

My World of Antiques

Collect, buy and sell everyday antiques like an expert

HIGH LIFE HIGHLAND

3800 18 0080677 4	
Askews & Holts	18-Jan-2019
745.1	£20.00

WITHDRAWN

JOHN BLAKE

Published by John Blake Publishing,
2.25 The Plaza,
535 Kings Road,
Chelsea Harbour,
London SW10 0SZ

www.johnblakebooks.com

www.facebook.com/johnblakebooks ▪
twitter.com/jblakebooks ▪

First published in hardback in 2018

ISBN: 978-1-78606-475-2

All rights reserved. No part of this publication may be reproduced, stored in a retrieval system, or
transmitted in any form or by any means, without the prior permission in writing of the publisher, nor be
otherwise circulated in any form of binding or cover other than that in which it is published and without a
similar condition including this condition being imposed on the subsequent purchaser.

British Library Cataloguing-in-Publication Data:
A catalogue record for this book is available from the British Library.

Design by www.envydesign.co.uk
Typeset by www.glensaville.design

Printed and bound in Latvia

1 3 5 7 9 10 8 6 4 2

Text copyright © Paul Martin 2018

The right of Paul Martin to be identified as the author of this work has been asserted by him in accordance
with the Copyright, Designs and Patents Act 1988.

Papers used by John Blake Publishing are natural, recyclable products made from wood grown in sustainable
forests. The manufacturing processes conform to the environmental regulations of the country of origin.

Every reasonable effort has been made to trace copyright-holders of material reproduced in this book,
but if any have been inadvertently overlooked the publishers would be glad to hear from them.

John Blake Publishing is an imprint of Bonnier Books UK
www.bonnierbooks.co.uk

CONTENTS

FOREWORD

by Sir Peter Blake

As I write this foreword to Paul Martin's book, it has just passed midnight, and it's my birthday and I'm eighty-six today. I have been collecting for seventy-three years.

I was seven years old when the Second World War began and almost everything was soon in short supply, so as a child I was in no position to collect anything. I was evacuated twice and then, in 1945, returned to Dartford, obtained a place at Gravesend School of Art and became an art student at the age of thirteen.

Gravesend had a wonderful junkyard next to the railway station. On my first visit I bought a naïve painting of the liner *Queen Mary*, a papier-mâché Victorian tray and a leather-bound set of Shakespeare plays – my years of collecting had begun.

Paul Martin is probably best known for his role as the presenter of *Flog It!*, but he is also a collector and lover of antiques and it's fascinating to read about his collections. What a wonderful job, to have a constant stream of people showing you their treasures and learning all the time about antiques and fascinating objects.

INTRODUCTION

I love my job. Despite the fact that it takes me away from my family and involves a huge amount of travelling, I count myself lucky in being able to combine my passion for antiques with making *Flog It!* and meeting so many people who share my enthusiasm. *Flog It!* ran for the best part of twenty years and the show has taken me all over the country from Belfast and Inverness to Dover and Devon. We have made more than a thousand shows and I will admit that different venues in different towns can tend to meld into each other in my mind, but all I have to do is look at a photo or a film clip and memories from that venue come flooding back. The people are what make the difference. Seeing faces helps to place a venue in my head because the people who come along to a day out at a *Flog It!* valuation are what make it all so special. They are hugely patient when they are waiting to sit down at one of the valuation tables with our experts, and I try to talk to as many of them as possible while they are waiting. The antiques and artefacts that they bring along to the show are often quite remarkable, but it's the people themselves that I find amazing.

When people bring precious family heirlooms along to be valued, the stories behind those pieces are always fascinating – little slices of history that are unique and wonderful. Being able to verify the history and provenance of a piece adds enormously to its value, although sometimes the story behind an object is more interesting than the piece itself. Some visitors may leave a little disappointed when it turns out that Granddad's war medals aren't worth as much as they had hoped, but our experts will at least have given them a little extra insight into their family treasures. Yet, as often as not, our guests are pleasantly surprised by the valuation of the items they have brought along, be they jewellery, paintings, furniture, glassware or childhood toys. Not everyone wants to 'flog' what they bring along, but I am always intrigued to hear what people who do decide to sell want to do with the proceeds. Sometimes family heirlooms are of too much sentimental value ever to sell, but I love it when people who bought a piece years ago simply because they liked it decide to sell, especially if they want to use the money they raise to go out and acquire another antique.

That can become addictive, although no one should ever be afraid of selling an antique in order to 'trade up' to something else, perhaps something of better quality and more expensive. Trading up allows you to move up through the market, gradually acquiring more valuable pieces. I always like to get my hands on the best pieces that I can afford – be it a stick-back chair, a chest of drawers or a lovely example of taxidermy – because so much at the top end of the market sells for prices that are way beyond my means.

When we had finished the landmark thousandth episode of *Flog It!*, I thought it was time for a pat on the back. 'Treat yourself, Paul,' I thought. 'That's quite an achievement.'

So off I went to Christie's auction house in South Kensington. It was preview day, and I took my son, Dylan, because up for grabs in the sale was a 10-million-year-old fossilised skull of a triceratops, a Victorian stuffed ostrich and the skeleton of a cave bear standing on its hind legs, which looked absolutely terrifying! Dill loves all things quirky and there was plenty there for all to see and touch. Yes, no barriers – this is an auction room, after all, where potential buyers can handle the goods, not a museum with laser alarms and barriers. And, believe me, we got hands-on. It was wonderful. With a sale guide of £15,000 to £20,000, the 126,000-year-old cave bear eventually sold for £35,000. It was totally, totally out of my league, but we just had to see it and marvel in awe at the world that once was. On the day, the triceratops skull sold for more than £190,000, a real bargain in my books. After all, where would you find another piece like it, a one-off sculptural piece of natural history, very on-trend at present and very cool, unique and individual?

Whether you are selling in order to trade up, or simply shopping for a piece of furniture, auction houses are wonderful places to find things that will look wonderful in your home – and you can save the planet at the same time. Antiques are, after all, incredibly 'green' with the lowest of carbon footprints. A Georgian chest of drawers will have been

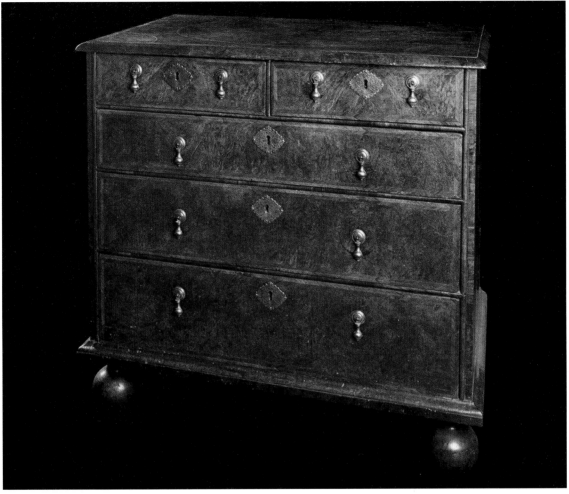

An example of Georgian furniture.

produced in a workshop in daylight – or by candlelight – without the use of power tools, and it will have been serving its purpose for more than two hundred years. Yet Georgian furniture has never been cheaper. Now is a great time to buy as, not only does it look fabulous, it features superb craftsmanship and it will last your entire lifetime – and your kids' lifetimes, too. Why buy a modern piece of mass-produced furniture from a department-store chain when you could have something like that for roughly the same price?

Of course, an antique piece can also be a strong investment for the future – especially if you're lucky enough to find something with provenance – proof of its history that places all fine art and antiques in the right place at the right time and shows that it is precisely what it purports to be. If you find something that was once owned by someone famous or that belonged to a great country house or institution, it could have a connection to a historical event. Look out for accompanying photographs of it *in situ*, paperwork, receipts, dates, signatures, invoices and auction catalogues. Do some research. It will all help to add value and tell a story of our magnificent heritage – a window into the past. Of course, even someone like me, who is supposed to know what he's doing, can come unstuck, as I did when trying to buy a bookcase that once belonged to Winston Churchill. You'll read all about that later.

I did manage to find my celebratory treat in the end – another primitive Windsor stick-back chair. These chairs are my fix; I'm addicted to them; I have particular favourites and, if you know what to look out for and you get it right, it will put a smile on your face for ever. If you go antique hunting with an open mind, even with a limited budget, you'll never be disappointed. There

are a thousand ways of seeing something, and in this book I hope to help you look at things in a different light and buy with confidence. If I can pass on a few tips and encourage you to go antique hunting, hopefully you will come to love the antiques world as much as I do, and together we can have fun keeping our history and heritage alive for future generations.

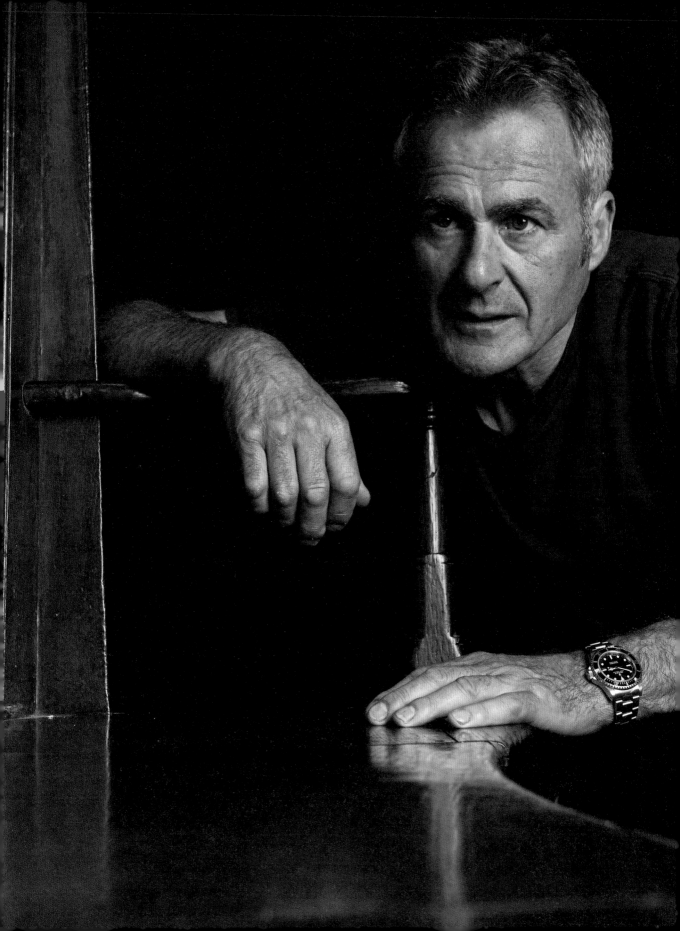

WHAT MAKES A GOOD DEALER

As a dealer, I've always been a one-man band. I've been dealing in antiques since well before my career in television began, and, up until fifteen years before writing this book, I couldn't imagine doing anything else. Even now, with more than a thousand episodes of *Flog It!* under my belt, I still consider myself very much in the trade, albeit in the guise of a television antiques presenter. And nowadays, of course, I am involved in the trade as a collector rather than a dealer. There is a subtle difference. As a collector, I now enjoy the luxury of hanging on to the pieces that I buy rather than always trading onwards and upwards, but dealing is still where my heart lies.

I suppose you could say that dealing in antiques runs in the blood. My uncle was a dealer, and as a young lad I was always fascinated by the idea of collecting. It started with the Brooke Bond tea cards; the anticipation and excitement as Mum opened a new packet of teabags is as fresh in my mind now as it was then. There were lots of different sets to collect – 'British Costume', 'Flags and Emblems of the World' or 'Transport Through the Ages'. I remember it so well: would the box contain the card I needed to add to my set, or just another card that I already had, one to swap at school? Such wonderful, happy memories – and, when I think about it, I can still smell the tea. Ironically, I don't drink tea these days and, if I do, it's Earl Grey, but I suppose taste in hot drinks is just as subject to change as taste in collectibles.

The kings and queens of England were the next to hold my fancy. I accrued stamps from the Royal Philatelic Collection, which is widely regarded as the world's finest and most comprehensive collection of British postal stamps. The collection includes stamps from the very beginnings of the modern British postal system in the 1800s and journeys through the ages, brushing across the reign of every monarch from Queen Victoria to Queen Elizabeth II and housing some of the rarest stamps in history.

In among the kings and queens, I was the proud owner of many of the stamps from the pioneer airmail flights to Canada, all firmly glued into their correct

albums so there could be no chance of their being lost. Unfortunately, I later found that in my enthusiasm I had been slightly overzealous with my use of the glue, and all the pages had rippled and undulated through the album! As I have since discovered, gluing the stamps in place was not an ideal approach in the first place. If you find yourself the owner of any historical stamps, never glue them down, as their value will drop by 70 per cent. I should have secured individual stamps in the album using stamp hinges – little pieces of gummed paper that are folded in half and lightly moistened, with one half then stuck to the album page and one half stuck to the back of the stamp. These cause little or no damage to the stamp, although modern self-adhesive mounts are even better.

You do have to be very careful about keeping stamps and your stamp albums somewhere dry so that the stamps or the album pages won't get damp. Moisture can cause all sorts of damage to the stamps, including making them stick themselves to the album pages. Even the most valuable of stamps, such as the Penny Black, have the gum still left on the back, and these were the focus of my next collecting venture.

Oh, the excitement of finding something new! When I was a lad the Penny Black was talked about with great reverence: the world's first adhesive postage stamp, the Holy Grail of all stamp collections. As a twelve-year-old who had listened to adults referring to the stamp time and again, I got it into my head that there was only one, but experience soon put paid to that assumption. The stamp was first issued on 1 May 1840 and there were a great many of them – more than 68 million! Nowadays, their value depends on condition and rarity. A Penny Black in good condition might sell for a few hundred pounds, whereas Penny Blacks in mint condition can sell for many thousands of pounds. The stamps were printed in sheets that were not perforated, so you had to cut your stamp from the sheet using scissors. Penny Blacks that were neatly cut, with an even margin around the stamp, are worth more than those that were cut by someone with poor eyesight or a shaky hand! Scarcity and imperfections add worth to the most valuable among them.

A prime example of imperfections adding value lies in some printings of the Penny Red. This is the stamp that replaced the Penny Black in 1841. The red colour made it easy to see black-ink cancellation marks on the stamp, making it more difficult for anyone to reuse it. Like the Penny Black, the Penny Red was printed in sheets – at first even using the same printing plates but applying red ink instead of black – and initially the sheets

had no perforations. When it was decided that perforations would be a good idea, so that stamps could easily be torn from a sheet, they had a few technical problems. A fault with a misaligned printing plate meant that, when the printed sheets of stamps went through the perforating machine, the inaccurate printing meant that the perforations were lined up incorrectly. The problem was spotted and all but one of the test sheets were destroyed. The errant test sheet became sought after by stamp collectors the world over, and in 2012 a single Penny Red from that sheet sold for £550,000. In general, however, the Penny Red is worth less than the Penny Black, partly because so many of them were produced. It was on sale for thirteen years as opposed to the Penny Black's nine months, and many billions were printed. As for me, I soon shifted by focus from stamps, moving on to coins, although the Penny Red still holds my interest today.

So, after all of that, we come to the inevitable: what does it take to become a good dealer? What must you do to move beyond the realms of the amateur collector and launch into a successful career?

First and foremost, you've got to follow your instincts and learn to trust them. A good dealer will see the personality in an object as well as its function and the skill and craftsmanship that may have gone into making it. Your own eyes and your instinct will help you to appreciate a standout piece that has journeyed through the pages of history, a window into the past. Personality will make an object attractive, but you must look for quality in the item, as this is the most important characteristic it can have. A good way to learn what to look for in determining the quality of any piece is to spend time with specialist dealers in your field of collecting. What do they look for in an antique? Most experts are happy to share their knowledge and help to promote that whole antiques industry. Look, listen and learn all you can from them.

Another hugely enjoyable part of the learning process is in regularly visiting museums and historic houses. The stories of the building and the objects within it will likely intertwine – learn to feel the tales they tell. You should also become a regular visitor to your local auction rooms – and even those that are not so local. Get to know when the regular auctions are held, examine their lists and get hands-on. You can learn a lot from comparing the description of an item in a list or catalogue to the item itself. Talk to the staff and auctioneers and get to know them, too, seeking their tips and advice.

Go online, read books and get up and investigate. There is an enormous amount of information available on the Internet. Local libraries are excellent places to do some research, especially if you are investigating something that has been produced in that area. Play the detective and try to be a pioneer, establishing your own tastes and values.

All of this will help you become passionate about the items you buy, and will ultimately help you to sell them. And sell them you must. Though it is easy to grow attached you cannot just collect and hoard your best items, as this will not win you success as a dealer. Passing some of your best finds to your clients will help you develop a good reputation as well as a loyal client base. This in turn will help you discover new things. Chatting to clients, or potential clients, is a great way to learn by word of mouth that 'Mrs Brown has one just like this that she's been talking about selling.'

You may well need to travel around to do your research or to follow up leads. It is important that you be prepared to get in the car and drive for hours. Accepting that you will need to do this and having the right attitude towards it is vital as it will give you the strength and energy to keep on going! Enjoy it – treat it as a day out, seeing somewhere different and meeting different people.

Familiarise yourself with the industry. Get to know trade bodies such as BADA (British Antique Dealers' Association) and LAPAD (Labelling, Advertising and Promotion Advice Division) and their rules and regulations – and always abide by those rules. Now more than ever it is so important to be honest. The Internet has revolutionised selling, making it possible to purchase an item from anywhere in the world at the click of a mouse or the press of a button, simply based on a photograph and a description. Distance means the Internet buyer needs to feel able to purchase with confidence, so a good dealer must, above all, be honest if they are to be successful. While it is now easier than ever to establish a good reputation with a wide client base, it is easier still to establish a bad one. Remember that, as a dealer, you are an expert in what you do, not simply a tradesman, and this means you need to be patient, generous and creative with your items rather than constantly pushing for a sale.

Finally, enjoy the unpredictability of one day to another. Of course, the uncertainty must be controlled to a degree, but you cannot have power over everything. Go with your gut and see where it takes you and, as always, be the eternal optimist. You never know what you may find.

A VISIT TO DUMFRIES HOUSE

It is amazing what can happen in the space of twenty-four hours. Sitting at home with my wife Charlotte at nine o'clock one evening, glass of wine in hand, I reflected on the day I'd just had and started to wonder if it had all actually happened, or if I had possibly just nodded off and dreamt it! Even by the standards of a TV presenter, used to dashing around the country, meeting lots of interesting people and seeing some amazing things, my day had been remarkable. I was struggling to put it into words and tell Charlotte all about it, as I couldn't quite bridge the gaping chasm between then and only a few hours before without it all sounding like a complete fantasy.

It was 2011. We were in the middle of filming for *Britain's Hidden Heritage*, a series for BBC1, and I had just had the rare opportunity and incredible privilege of meeting with the Prince of Wales at the world-famous Dumfries House in Ayrshire, Scotland.

Dumfries House stands proudly amid formal gardens surrounded by an extensive estate just west of the town of Cumnock. The house was built between 1754 and 1759 by the 5th Earl of Dumfries, William Dalrymple-Crichton. Having resigned his commission in the army, the earl settled with his wife on the estate in the mid-1740s and later began planning a brand-new house. The most celebrated Scottish architect of the time, William Adam, had died in 1748 but his three sons, John, Robert and James, had taken over the family business, with Dumfries House becoming their first major project. The Adams' drawings, mainly the designs of Robert, who was the most talented architect, were submitted to the earl in 1754, showing a Palladian-style house with a three-storey main building linked to two pavilions. The house is really very much as William Adam himself might have designed it. He favoured the elegant, symmetrical Palladian style, named after Venetian architect Andrea Palladio, and the exterior of Dumfries House is hugely impressive, although not overly ornate.

Sadly for the earl, his wife died in 1755 while the house was still under construction, but he forged ahead with the building, ensuring that his own taste and style were reflected in the Adam brothers' interiors. The brothers were not, however, the only ones employed by the earl to make the inside of his home look modern, lavish and enormously impressive.

His plan was for the house to acquire a

Dumfries House in all its glory.

reputation as one of Scotland's finest, most beautiful grand residences. That way he hoped to entice a new wife to the estate in order that he could have children (his only son had died at the age of nine) to whom he could pass his estate and title. Only the most fashionable décor and furnishings would do, so he commissioned furniture from Edinburgh craftsmen William Mathie, Alexander Peter and Francis Brodie. But the thing I found most exciting was the amazing collection of furniture

that the earl commissioned from the man who was, at that time, seriously trendy: Thomas Chippendale.

Chippendale was a Yorkshireman, the son of a woodworker. He had trained as a cabinetmaker in York and in London, where he eventually started his own business. In 1754 he published the first edition of his *The Gentleman and Cabinet-Maker's Director*, which was basically a catalogue of his furniture designs, illustrated with intricate drawings of individual pieces as well as technical drawings showing how they were made. Of course, that gave every other furniture maker in the country, and abroad, the chance to copy what Chippendale was doing, but it also brought orders flooding in for his furniture.

Chippendale did not only create furniture, but also worked as an interior designer. He collaborated with Robert Adam on a number of projects, designing furniture and colour schemes to suit rooms, and rooms to fit

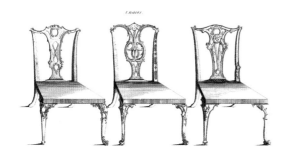

An illustration from Chippendale's seminal catalogue, *The Gentleman and Cabinet-Maker's Director*.

furnishings. Dumfries House was one of the first of more than two dozen commissions at stately homes all over Britain where Chippendale's furniture constituted a major part of the interior design. It's not surprising, then, that Dumfries House became home to a unique collection of Chippendale's work. The Earl of Dumfries visited Chippendale's London showroom early in 1759 and, a few months later, thirty-nine crates of furniture

were delivered to Dumfries House. What is surprising is that the furnishings stayed in the house for more than two hundred years. I couldn't believe that I was to have the chance to see it all up close – Dumfries House had never previously been open to the public – especially as the collection was all so nearly sold off at auction and scattered to the four winds.

What had happened was that William Dalrymple-Crichton, the 5th Earl, succeeded in his plan to attract a new wife, marrying a distant cousin, Anne Duff, in 1762. They had no children, however, and, when the earl died in 1768, the house, estate and title passed to his nephew, Patrick McDouall-Crichton. On McDouall-Crichton's death, John Crichton-Stuart became the 7th Earl of Dumfries, with the title, the house and the estate staying in the Crichton-Stuart family right into the twenty-first century. Up to 1993, the grandmother of the current Earl of Dumfries had lived in Dumfries House but, when she died, he decided that the house had to be sold. He needed to concentrate family resources on other important properties such as Mount Stuart House on the Isle of Bute; he is also Marquess of Bute. It was offered to the National Trust but negotiations eventually faltered and, in April 2007, it was announced that the house and estate would be sold, with the contents of the house to be auctioned separately.

It was then that the Prince of Wales decided that he needed to try to do something to save this wonderful house and its collection of furniture for the nation, but he had very little time to raise the finance required to stop the whole lot going on the open market. At one stage, lorries full of Chippendale furniture were already on the road, heading to auction at Christie's in London. So how did Prince Charles manage to rescue this historic house, which came perilously close to being lost forever? I needed to know more.

I was picked up bright and early and driven to Heathrow prior to flying up to Scotland on the day I was to interview Prince Charles. At Heathrow I met our production team, who were already kitted out in their finest suits, and we casually sat and ate breakfast at the airport. For my part, I didn't dare change into my own suit until I was safely inside the walls of Dumfries House. I couldn't bear the thought of interviewing the Prince of Wales (also known in Scotland as the Duke of Rothesay) with eggy breakfast stains on my jacket or my trousers all crumpled from the journey. Having touched down at Glasgow Airport, we were driven to Dumfries House, where the prince would soon be arriving. It didn't occur to me to feel nervous as I stared

A serpentine Chippendale commode.

out of the window on our approach to the house. I was admiring the sprawling, two-thousand-acre estate while we drove towards the building itself, with its grand entrance set at the top of an impossibly wide flight of stairs. But it was the servants' entrance that we were to be ushered in through, and we stepped quietly through a side door into the past.

Far from being an anticlimax, the inside of the house was, if anything, more remarkable than its exterior. Dumfries House has spent much of its life frozen in time – untouched and often unlived in – so much of the building still looked almost exactly the same as it did

Another Chippendale masterpiece, the Kenure Cabinet, worth £4 million.

Dumfries House's stunning Pewter Corridor, pictured above and overleaf.

when the Adam brothers finished building it.

Unlike many other such country homes that have been remodelled, redecorated and refurbished over the years, Dumfries still had nearly all of its original contents in their original settings, and it was this that made the place unique. I found myself thinking that, if the old 5th Earl were to walk through the hallways on the same day as I did, he wouldn't notice much amiss.

I met the restoration and cleaning staff, the loyal team who had been restoring the house to its beautiful, pristine condition for the previous three years and making it ready for visits from the public. Every day at 7 a.m. they begin with almost military precision, drawing up the curtains and dusting everything in sight. Guide John Morrison filled me in more on the house's fascinating history and showed me some of the breathtaking Chippendale furniture. There are only around six hundred fully authenticated pieces of Chippendale

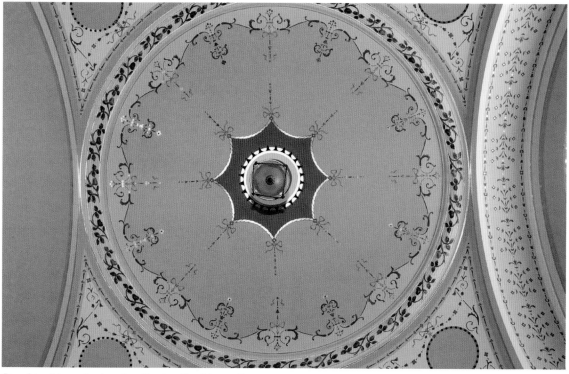

Dumfries House's stunning Pewter Corridor ceiling

furniture in the world and more than fifty of those are in Dumfries House, all with the original invoices to prove their provenance and authenticity. In the Blue Drawing Room there are the most incredible Chippendale elbow chairs and sofas upholstered in a blue damask patterned silk. Against one wall is the famous rosewood bookcase. It is the only one of its kind in existence and is described by Thomas Chippendale on the original invoice as 'Rosewood Bookcase with carved and gilt ornament on the top and doors, a writing drawer in the underpart and a clothes press and drawers at each end'. The original invoice

price was £47.5s – that's £47.25! When it was due for auction in 2007 it was expected to fetch anything up to £4 million and is now estimated to be worth up to £12 million.

Finally, it was time for the prince to arrive. I met first with his personal assistant, who introduced herself and briefly explained about Prince Charles's arrival. I was to call him 'Your Royal Highness' in the first instance, after which I could refer to him as 'Prince Charles'. The helicopter bringing him in arrived on time shortly thereafter, but the interview was put back an hour as he needed a rest, followed by tea and biscuits! In the meantime, we ran

Dumfries House's prize piece: a £12 million rosewood bookcase.

through our marks and positions for filming. I was ordered to stick closely to the six questions we had previously discussed and was strictly forbidden to ask his Royal Highness anything else while on camera. All was well; I still didn't feel any trace of nerves and was perfectly in control. My director and crew were flapping about with last-minute checks – and then in walked Prince Charles.

That was it – instantly, my legs went to jelly. I had only six questions and yet I was forgetting them all! What was I going to do if my mind went blank during the interview? I needn't have worried because Prince Charles is utterly professional when it comes to these things and was very friendly. What's more, he'd done his homework – on me! He enquired about my family, asked after my German Shepherd by name (How was Bluebelle? he wanted to know), and we quickly moved on to discussing our shared admiration for Welsh furniture and, naturally, the refined craftsmanship of Thomas Chippendale.

We were actually standing in the family bedroom (one of around twenty bedrooms in the house), which may sound like an odd place to meet but, back in the eighteenth century, this would have been used as a reception room as well as a place to sleep. The rosewood bookcase was originally in this room and I was chatting to Prince Charles beside the most incredible four-poster bed – the single most expensive item ordered from Thomas Chippendale by the 5th Earl. The bed has a beautifully carved mahogany frame hung with 130 yards (119 metres) of the same blue damask silk, imported from Genoa, that adorns the elbow chairs in the Blue Drawing Room. It took two years to restore the bed, mainly because the dome and the headboard, which are carved pine, have a very special alternative to paint or polish. They are covered with the blue silk fabric that is stretched over the wood, worked into every detail of the carving and glued into place. The

bed is a work of art, but comfortable as well. The mattress has three layers: horse hair on the bottom, wool in the middle and a top layer of Danzig feathers for that luxurious feather-bed snooze, although I didn't try it out!

Above the mantelpiece in front of which we were standing, there is a fabulously ornate Chippendale carved chimney overmantle, beautifully gilded, with mirror glass in the lower section and the upper part inset with a hand-knotted carpet panel. The panel shows a colourful, detailed scene of flowers tumbling out of a basket and was created by Thomas Moore. Moore was England's most renowned carpet maker until Thomas Whitty of Axminster came along – and we were standing on one of the oldest Axminster carpets in existence! This preliminary chat passed by very pleasantly, but all at once it was time to begin the interview. All cameras on us, I asked my first question: the question that would surely have been on everyone's lips, had they been given the chance to ask it.

'How close did we come to losing Dumfries House and its collection of furniture?'

'It was a very close-run thing,' Prince Charles replied, before detailing the story of the furniture's rescue, which took place in the middle of the night with only hours to spare. His answers were long, thoughtful

and measured and it was safe to say that, within minutes, I was in awe of the man. He spoke softly but it was obvious that he meant what he was saying, that he really did believe in the importance of preserving our history. It transpired that, when he first heard about the house's imminent demise, he had put together a consortium to raise the £45 million pounds it would take to save it and keep it for the nation. At the time, £12 million had already been committed, and over the previous months Prince Charles had worked to raise this sum to 25 million. The remaining £20 million was loaned by the prince's own charity, the My Charities Foundation, through which he took the monumental risk of borrowing the required money from the bank.

Amazed, I asked him how he had set about bringing the house back to life and what he had learned during the process. He detailed practical issues such as heating and electricity alongside more specialist matters, which required teams of experts in textiles, conservation and furniture. Twenty million pounds was a lot of money for the house to recoup, I thought, and, sure enough, he went on to tell me how he planned to attract paying visitors to the estate. His idea of 'heritage-led regeneration' held my interest, and, when I asked him to elaborate, he outlined his plans to have Dumfries House not only pay for its own upkeep, but also to benefit the area that surrounded it. His hope was that a new and thriving community would be built around the house.

My interview was not yet over. Now for a question that seemed simple, but was deceptively complex.

'What is heritage?'

Of course, he could answer the question perfectly.

'More than anything, I suppose, our heritage is a physical manifestation of our roots and of our culture,' he began, and I listened intently as he described the importance of heritage in telling our cultural story.

There was time left for one final question.

'Should our attitude to preserving the past change during a time of austerity?'

A thought-provoking question, and one I thought I knew the answer to.

'Absolutely not – quite the opposite,' he began, then explained his vision of historic places offering not only artistic and cultural

value but also economic benefits. I couldn't help but agree with him. If anything, he said, it was during times of austerity that heritage-led regeneration projects such as the one at Dumfries House could make a real difference. The work that has gone into the project is proving to be of benefit to the local community in very real terms, creating jobs and bringing visitors to the area who spend money locally. Dumfries House and Estate is now open to the public and is a venue for weddings and other special events. There is now a restaurant, a walled garden, a twenty-two-room hotel in The Lodge and Valentine's Education Farm, where children can learn about food and horticulture, as well as a host of other attractions. The prince's foundation has also been responsible for a new open-air swimming pool at nearby New Cumnock and Knockroon, a sustainable housing development. It just goes to show what you can achieve in a relatively short space of time if you have the vision and determination of the Prince of Wales!

All too soon, the interview and my big day out were over. Within hours I was back at home with the family after just another day at the office, with time on my hands to reflect. In a career filled with beautiful discoveries and incredible people, this is still by far one of the most memorable moments I have ever experienced. But that's one of the great things about this job and why I enjoy what I do: you never know what's around the corner.

CHIPPENDALE

In the eighteenth century, the average life expectancy in Britain had 'risen' to around forty years of age, which, considering that it's around eighty-two today, helps us to appreciate the tough lives our ancestors lived. Of course, there were some who made it past the age of forty, and anyone who knows their kings and queens knows that the Georges (I, II and III), who ruled through most of that century, lived to be much older. George I made it to sixty-seven, George II was seventy-six and George III, despite his madness, lived to the ripe old age of eighty-one. You need to know a bit about history and the monarchy when you are working with antiques and I have learned a lot over the years, although I will admit that it can get a bit confusing, especially when foreign royalty becomes involved, so, if I am presenting a piece to camera, I still like to check my facts just to be sure!

Georges I, II and III, however, led lives of great privilege and comfort, unlike the majority of their poor subjects. For most of Britain's commoners, life was pretty grim. The most basic things, such as clean drinking water, were often hard to come by. Water in towns came from rivers or streams that were polluted with rubbish and sewage and were filthy beyond belief. Poor sanitation and dirty water caused epidemics of life-threatening illnesses such as dysentery and cholera, so people drank ale or cider in preference to water, as boiling and fermentation killed off the bacteria that caused diseases, although people didn't really understand that at the time. All they knew was that ale and cider were better to drink than water.

Used in excess, alcohol also helped to obliterate the grind and the distress of everyday life, and for many it was gin, which became known as 'Mother's Ruin', that was the alcohol of choice. Prostitution was rife, as were petty crime and assault, while hanging by the neck until dead was a common form of punishment, even for offences as petty as stealing an apple or strange things such as 'being in the company of Gypsies for a month'. At one time there were more than 220 offences for which you could be hanged.

As people poured into the cities to seek their fortunes, or simply in search of jobs and a predominantly deluded perception of a better life, they were packed into dilapidated hovels where entire families would live and sleep in one room. Abuse, neglect and sexually transmitted diseases were commonplace, and, for the average man, the only way to clamber up the social ladder was to join the army or navy or go into service on one of the great country estates, such as West Wycombe Park, Chatsworth or Bowood.

For women, there were far fewer opportunities, with 'service' as one of the only hopes of self-improvement, although many clung to the hope of finding a moneyed suitor as their route out of poverty. Snaring a rich husband, or at the very least a man with good prospects, was the dream ticket for some girls. For both sexes, there was also the church, but becoming a priest or a nun wasn't to everyone's taste. One thing that young people three hundred years ago certainly had in common with youngsters today was that there was a good living to be had in learning a trade. An apprenticeship might mean the possibility of eventually joining the ranks of the ever-expanding middle and merchant classes. Get yourself a trade and you were set for life – the kind of young man with good prospects that attracted the

Chippendale furniture on display at Burton Constable Hall.

ladies. There were a few female apprentices in some trades, but, in eighteenth century London, it has been estimated that only around 1 per cent of apprentices were girls. This was a man's world.

Yet an apprenticeship was no joyride. The life of an apprentice was hard, with beatings the likely result of any minor transgression or for failing to learn quickly enough. One of the great furniture designers, examples of some of whose chairs are on display at Stourhead House in Wiltshire, had a fearful reputation as an aggressive bully. One of his apprentices actually took out a lawsuit against him after he received a thrashing. The defendant's name was Giles Grendey and his chairs were richly coloured, intricately carved and sought after to this day. But talk about an overbearing artistic temperament!

Grendey was originally from Gloucestershire and lived from 1693 until 1780 – another Georgian gentleman who lived to a fine age. Perhaps Grendey's own life as an apprentice made him tough enough to live longer. It would certainly have taught him that harsh treatment was the normal order, with corporal punishment considered quite acceptable at a time when domestic abuse didn't even register as a crime. Appalling, to say the least. Grendey was apprenticed to a London woodworker, William Sherborne, in the early years of the eighteenth century but had his own apprentices by 1726 and a workshop in the Covent Garden area, before moving to larger premises in St John's Square, Clerkenwell, in 1772.

While history shows us that he had a nasty streak running through his veins, his work is best known because he added a 'Makers Label', often initialling pieces as well. He had a successful export business with a suite of around eighty pieces of furniture, including chairs, tables, mirrors, desks and bookcases, ordered in the 1730s by the Duke of Infantado for his palace in Lazcano in northern Spain. A fire at Grendey's Covent Garden workshop in 1731 was reported in the newspapers at the time as having destroyed furniture worth around £1,000, which was a breathtaking sum of money at the time, especially when you think that more than eighty per cent of families in the country had a total yearly income under £50. Most survived on less than half of that.

For the moneyed classes and the aristocracy, gated away in their opulent estates, the world was a very different place. They enjoyed wine from Italy, Spain and France, bottles shipped in from Madeira, silks and tapestries from the Continent, fine furniture and architects to design the homes in which they were displayed. With wealth came education. With education came a thirst for knowledge and with knowledge came a desire to experience the world, and so along came the Grand Tour (more of which later) and the influences of the neo-Classical. By neo-Classical we mean Ancient Greece and Rome and, to a lesser degree, the Moorish architecture of Spain and the Ottoman Empire. We mean huge sculptures, columns and triangular porticos and façades, rich colours and textures.

It became terribly trendy – a way of flaunting your wealth and intellect – to have ancient sculptures and carvings on display in your home. To meet the aspirations of the wealthy elite, ruined temples and palaces were stripped of their art by the likes of Lord Elgin, whose plunder of the Acropolis in Athens causes controversy to this day. It is shocking to think that, between 1801 and 1812, having struck a deal with officials of the Ottoman Empire, which ruled Greece at the time, Lord Elgin removed half of the existing sculptures from the Parthenon and two other buildings on the Acropolis site. There was a huge furore about this plunder and questions were asked in Parliament at the time, although Elgin was found to have done nothing illegal. He was persuaded to sell the 'Elgin Marbles' to the British

One of the Elgin Marbles – a great, if controversial, treasure of the British Museum.

Government and they were ultimately put on display in the British Museum in London, where they remain to this day. When they became independent from the Ottoman Empire in 1832, the Greeks asked for their sculptures back. It really is a scandal that no real progress has been made towards returning them. The Greeks are still asking.

As the moneyed classes' craving for Palladian architecture grew, they began to employ architects such as the Adam brothers, who, like all fine architects catering to clients of taste, worked hand in hand with interior furnishers and cabinetmakers. Often, pieces of furniture were made specifically by cabinetmakers such as Grendey and Chippendale to mirror and match the coving and plasterwork. Once a house had been designed or redesigned and embellished, the owner would start to amass collections and, of course, buy more and more furniture, more paintings and more of just about everything.

With an army of servants to wash, mend, polish and clean his house and prepare his food, the estate owner would want for little, and his chances of living a long life increased, although ailments commonly chased away with antibiotics today weren't too fussed about choosing their victims on the grounds of wealth or status. Of course, with a clean house, floors scrubbed daily with soap and water and clothes that were brushed and pressed daily, the mould and filth prevalent in the squalid homes of the poor had been banished. If you had money, you could live a healthier life.

The aristocracy, however, were as likely to drink themselves to death as the working classes, while the ever-expanding middle classes, although hardly exempt from vices and debauchery, were inclined to follow a more wholesome lifestyle, observant of religion, temperance and cleanliness. This rising class of merchants, tradesmen and businesspeople were, in fact, aspiring to emulate a ruling class of whom they knew little. Today, this might seem like a confused world, yet this was the forward-thinking, enterprising Britain that had cut itself such a huge piece of the global pie through colonisation that, by the nineteenth century, it would paint much of the globe pink, the official mapping colour of the British Empire. Through colonisation so many goods flooded into Britain from all over the world – from the Americas and the Caribbean, from Africa and India, from the Far East and Australia – that at one point 40 per cent of the world's trade was passing through Liverpool docks alone!

This meant that there was plenty of cash sloshing around among the emerging, upwardly mobile, middle class who had a desperate need to buy exquisite things to show off their newfound wealth. While many may have understood the basics of form, function and design, this aspirational new elite needed someone to explain high taste and style, just as fashionable people today are influenced by the styles and designs of others. The catalyst of style came from all over the empire and the myriad trade routes that had opened up, resulting in an influx of exotic goods into ports such as Liverpool, Glasgow and London.

Britain exported huge amounts of wool textiles during this period and ships returning empty would often use mahogany and exotic timbers as ballast. At first, this timber may simply have been left on the quayside, where it would have been chopped up and burned, but then, as they became aware of it, it was picked up by carvers. They quickly realised that these exotic timbers carved beautifully. Their close grain made them an ideal material with which to make furniture and into which they could carve intricate patterns. Mahogany was ideal: it lacked voids and pockets and resisted rot in our damp climate. Mahogany is a tropical hardwood native to the Americas and was largely unknown to British craftsmen who were used to working with walnut, imported from Spain, the Netherlands, France and

It was once said that the sun never set on the British Empire (marked pink here).

Italy, or oak, which was the principal homegrown timber of choice.

Once mahogany had been accepted as a wonderfully versatile timber, it was soon in great demand and import duties became a source of concern to the furniture industry. Robert Walpole, the then prime minister, dropped the levy on imported timber in 1733, which, in effect, ushered in the age of mahogany and other tropical hardwoods such as teak, ebony and rosewood.

You're probably wondering at this point why this chapter is called 'Chippendale'. In essence, I wanted to set the scene of the period and create an understanding of where this cabinetmaker's extraordinary designs originated. I don't simply mean his imagination: I mean his influences, too. We touched upon some of his history in the chapter about Dumfries House but, to remind you, Thomas Chippendale was born in Otley in Yorkshire in 1718. He was the son of a joiner, which is by no means a lesser trade; his father was an experienced and trained carpenter proficient in making anything from window frames to basic furniture.

Thomas followed in the family tradition, which was natural given that he grew up around carpentry tools and wood, and it's clear he took an early interest in his father's

work. He was also well educated at grammar school, learning to count, read and write, a huge advantage to him in his later business life as fewer than half the population could read and write. On leaving school, he trained under the appropriately named Richard Wood of York, a joiner and cabinetmaker. After moving to London, Thomas married in 1748 and set up a small workshop in Covent Garden, before moving on to The Strand and, ultimately, St Martin's Lane. All these locations were within walking distance of one another and were a hotbed of furniture-making studios from Oxford Street and Soho to St Paul's Church yard, with many furniture and cabinetmakers working out of the stables in pubs! St Martin's Lane was an especially creative environment with furniture makers, engravers, artists and architects all working in the vicinity of the St Martin's Lane Academy, a college specialising in art and design.

As our story unfolds, I want to explain that Chippendale went through several phases in his life. Some aspects of his endeavours have left their mark on cabinetmaking to this day and, while I shall explore his great works and designs in a moment, we need to remember that Chippendale passed away in near poverty. His life was a thoroughfare of the extraordinary, right through to his losing hold of the reigns of his empire as it hit pitfalls from which he never really recovered.

In St Martin's Lane, Chippendale actually leased three houses. The Chippendale family lived in one, his workshop was next door, and next door to that lived James Rannie, an upholsterer and businessman from Edinburgh. Rannie had invested the money that allowed Chippendale to move into the three-storey St Martin's Lane buildings in 1754, and outside the workshop there hung a sign in the shape of a chair proclaiming it to be 'The Cabinet and Upholstery Warehouse'.

Although they were to remain in these premises for more than half a century, it was always far from easygoing. The company suffered its first setback in the spring of 1755, when a fire destroyed the

A green japanned serpentine clothes press, English, 1771. Made for Sir Rowland Winn, 5th Baronet (1739 - 1785).

This Chippendale commode, designed by Robert Adam for Syon House, reflects the room it was built for.

workshop building. You can hardly help thinking that a fire in a place like this was an accident just waiting to happen: with wood, wood shavings and sawdust in the workshops of the cabinetmakers, feathers and cloth in the upholsterers' workshops, and veneers, carpets, wallpaper and drapes stored in other rooms within the building, the company provided a one-stop shop for interior design, furniture and soft furnishings. Then there was varnish, paint and polish, and, of course, the whole place was lit by candles!

Thomas had insured the building, but there were more than forty people who worked there and twenty-two of his craftsmen lost their tools in the fire. Workmen were expected to supply their own tools in those days and there was no money to offer them replacements, so a public appeal was made to raise funds to allow the men to get back to work. There was another cash crisis in 1766, when Rannie died and his estate decided to liquidate his share of the business by auctioning off company assets. This left Thomas facing bankruptcy and his letters to clients, including MP Sir Rowland Winn (who was late in paying his bill), left them in no doubt that he was in dire straits. The aristocracy were not always prompt in paying tradesmen!

Despite this, Thomas was working on a commission from Lord Edwin Lascelles to create furniture for Harewood House near Leeds. Over ten years, the contracts with Harewood House would be worth £10,000, a staggering amount of money at that time. In the short term, though, he was still struggling to keep the wolf from the door. He was even fined for trying to smuggle sixty chair frames into England from France, having failed to pay the correct import duty, presumably having declared them to be timber, which would have been cheaper to import. The chair frames may have been subcontracted to a French cabinetmaker (it was common for furniture makers to subcontract big orders) or may have been less elaborate than Chippendale's own designs – cheaper chairs to be supplied to clients for servants' quarters, perhaps, but in the end the chairs were confiscated. Thomas's finances were eventually rescued by Thomas Haig, who was his bookkeeper. Haig had worked for James Rannie and had stayed with Chippendale after Rannie's death. Haig invested money, some of which may have

A wonderful side-by-side comparison between desks by Chippendale (*left*) and Grendey (*right*).

A Chippendale *Director* drawing showing a rococo-styled bed.

come from Rannie's widow, that put the business back in the black.

While celebrating the life and work of Thomas Chippendale Snr, I also need to mention the work of Thomas Chippendale Jnr, who took over the business when his father died and ended up in Wiltshire working out of the stable block at Stourhead House, which was owned by the Hoare family, high-class bankers. Also, we must draw attention to Matthias Darley, a draughtsman and engraver who is listed as living at the same address as Chippendale on The Strand. Darley was to work on many of the intricate drawings of Chippendale's designs. It should be noted, too, that Thomas Chippendale Jnr's drawings were exceptionally good, suggesting Matthias Darley had tutored him as there are no records of his studying draughtsmanship.

So, Thomas Chippendale is, in my opinion, the finest cabinetmaker who ever lived. I could leave it there but I want to look at the work he undertook and what, in essence, set him apart from people like Grendey. While Grendey produced some wonderful furniture, there are subtle differences that set Chippendale apart. Grendey's work is, however, easy to identify, not least because he attached a maker's label, and stamped each piece with either his own initials or those of the craftsman who had worked on it. Chippendale never did that, and that, along with his *Gentleman and Cabinet-Maker's Director*, first published in 1754, can make Chippendale's work difficult to identify because the design drawings in the *Director* made it easy for very talented craftsmen to copy everything that Chippendale did. That is why receipts, or bills of sale, or household accounts from major estates are utterly invaluable in establishing the provenance of pieces believed to be by Chippendale.

The extraordinary book of designs, so complex and thorough, so well executed, so beautifully created, became the benchmark of style for generations. Even in modern plastic design we see designers parody and mirror quirks of Chippendale. With 160 illustrations in the first edition (there were ultimately three), the *Director* cost three and a half guineas (a guinea was twenty-one shillings, a pound was twenty shillings), which was more than a month's wages for most ordinary people. For high-class clients and other furniture makers, however, the *Director* was a bargain. It was a work of art in its own right, the correct thing to be seen in every fashionable home, and Chippendale's *Director* took the world of cabinetry by storm! It had been created, it is said, with more funding from Chippendale's Scottish connections and it served as a calling card for what Chippendale could actually do. It was, in fact, the first catalogue of designs ever produced within the trade. Suddenly, a whole new clientele became aware of his work and, as a result, business boomed and his name became synonymous with Rococo style. The scrolls and scallops, the cheeky swags, the whole plethora of fabrics and braids, and the exquisite proportions were the talking point of high society.

Chippendale became the director of a serious business with between fifty and eighty people employed in the manufacture and delivery of his incredible furniture. With a huge percentage of world trade passing through Britain's ports, and the influx of Huguenots and other peoples from around the globe bringing new designs and ideas, Chippendale, living among the bustle of cosmopolitan London, made an immediate mental note of everything he saw. There was inspiration all around. His styles were many

CHIPPENDALE

French Chairs, with or without arms, and a variety of styles for Legs, and Horse Fire Screen

c

and varied but all followed one particular philosophy: form follows function.

Chippendale, Hepplewhite and Sheraton, all names I'm sure you know, produced catalogues of design. Yet Chippendale offered a multitude of styles. I remember meeting top London antique dealer Patrick Sandberg in Kensington Church Street a few years ago. Patrick explained how to spot Chippendale chairs — it's the finely carved, wonderfully yoked-back you want to look for — almost sculpted in, like a waist from the shoulders with a finely carved fretwork back or back splat. Chippendale's chairs were of finer proportions than Grendey's and his emphasis on form meant that his work sometimes followed a classical French line. Others were known as Chinese Chippendale and exuded oriental style. Then there were the bold, scrolled and impressive Baroque and, by contrast, the more simplistic work, highlighted with a myriad of woods. French taste was a huge influence, even though, politically, France remained the perennial foe.

At Syon House, just west of London, I met Lady Caroline Percy. Caroline is the elder sister of the Duke of Northumberland and one of Britain's top interior designers. We looked at some Chippendale pieces on bold legs that mirrored the exquisite Robert Adam plasterwork and coving – yes, Chippendale and Adam were that obsessive when it came to detail! The patterns in the inlay of the cabinet matched the colours of the room's décor almost perfectly. It was incredible to learn that some of the furniture had been made in the Chippendale workshop, delivered to Syon House, placed in position and had stood there for over two centuries. The colours would once have been vibrant and emotive but they had faded over time and were now subtle and muted.

I was amazed that what we were looking at had been chosen by the original purchaser perusing Chippendale's *Director*.

The basis of the Chippendale catalogue was to offer different designs, different styles, and say, 'Look, this is what we can do – you choose what you want.' Chinese and Japanese style also influenced Chippendale with imported silks, pottery and furniture in all likelihood providing the inspiration from which to create his designs. Look at the fretwork, the intricate carving and the joinery below and in Chinese

CHIPPENDALE

Ribband-back Chairs and Fire Screens

Chippendale – the square legs with applied fret carving and interlaced back splats. Look at the pierced corner brackets, too – indeed, all of the above engravings show very distinct Chippendale traits and they show, quite obviously, what Chippendale is trying to express; yet I must point out that, in the designs, the chairs have odd front legs.

This is not because they were made that way; they weren't. It's simply to show a design, to say, 'Look, you can have this chair back with this chair leg, or that chair leg.' Whether a customer had just returned from the Grand Tour or, indeed, had worked with the likes of Adam, the *Director* was there to show that Chippendale could provide them with whatever options they wanted, or some they might not even have imagined. It created a benchmark of design and Chippendale worked closely with clients to add a flavour of their individual taste, with everything, of course, crisply carved.

Chippendale brought comfort to chair design, too, and for the first time – save for some of the more eccentric designs of the William and Mary and early Georgian upholstered chairs – the public were at last offered a design for a chair in which you could relax.

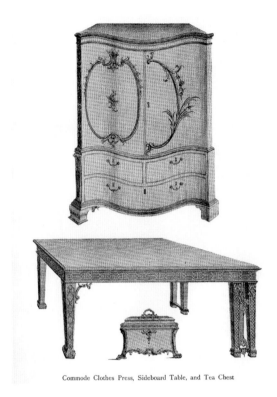

Commode Clothes Press, Sideboard Table, and Tea Chest

The legs of the table above, while in a traditional shape, offer a range of styles and designs, so a tapered leg need not be just a tapered leg: it might incorporate three legs or two legs and a lot of appliqué gilt all in one corner, or it might show bracketing with a French or Chinese influence.

The chest of drawers has a serpentine front with a wonderful curve reminiscent of the French designers whose work was so popular with British clients. The tea chest is more Rococo in style and, when we look at the ribbon back of the chairs above too, we see a mind that was receptive to style

and yet filled with a genius that added something unique. I don't think anyone can honestly say Chippendale emphasised any one point more than another. His was the eye of a man in control, the arbiter of taste. *The Gentleman and Cabinet-Maker's Director* ensured Chippendale his place in history and it's an interesting note to add that engravings from this tome turn up here and there, so do look out for them in salerooms and among ephemera dealers' stock.

Of course, the book of designs shared Chippendale's concepts with the colonies and, in America, the New England cabinetmakers' work of the period is sought after in its own right. Chippendale is copied in America and many pieces are of extremely high quality, but his designs were also copied in Dublin, Hamburg, Copenhagen and as far afield as India.

Old English and French Ornaments is a further catalogue of handles, appliqués and escutcheons and adornments published by Chippendale. I suppose by today's standards we might call this a little bit anal. I mean, seriously, how far can you go when designing a piece of furniture? In answer to that I'm guessing as far as Chippendale's imagination! Some of the French designs were very similar to Chippendale, so similar in fact that some people have suggested that

he copied things, lock, stock and barrel. Yet it became a matter of snobbery to have the best of Chippendale in one's house and, although Hepplewhite and Sheraton became ever more popular, Chippendale would enjoy a renaissance a hundred years later, when, once again, his designs took centre stage in the shop windows of London's West End.

If you've been to London, you've no doubt seen Nelson's Column standing in Trafalgar Square, and to the north side of the square you'll find the National Gallery, home to some of Britain's finest paintings. It was built forty-five years after Chippendale died and yet the stories meld together very nicely. The east wing is built on the site of a pauper's grave, which was on the periphery of St Martin-in-the-Fields. This is where Chippendale was buried. How fitting a site – a great artist buried beneath the work of other great artists. To me, looking at the National Gallery and knowing that Thomas is buried somewhere below, not far from his old workshops, somewhere that people go to indulge their love of art . . . Well, it would surely make him proud!

Some years ago I filmed a piece about Chippendale and stood outside his old workshop on St Martin's Lane. The building was being redeveloped, as is the trend in London, and the plaque that my producer had filmed earlier had, by now, been removed to the office of the architects. Looking through the gates of what so many millions of people must have walked and driven past without realising

Chippendale has had a profound effct on interior design ever since his heyday

the treasures that were created there was quite extraordinary. It struck me with, 'Why wasn't this sacred shrine to design and our heritage saved for the nation?' Truly, I felt sad seeing this important gateway to the past obliterated from London's landscape. His workshop may be gone and his grave built over, but, while nothing physically marks Chippendale's passing, his art, his accomplishment in design and everything he made are still celebrated and appreciated the world over.

I could, in reality, make a whole series and write an entire book about Chippendale, yet this is my little shrine to Thomas, my fan chapter, my eulogy and my respect all rolled into one. If it enthuses just one reader to learn more about this legend and his work, then I will consider it a privilege to have helped them on their way. I have sold Chippendale style and design, I've examined it and had the honour of exploring the carving and marquetry.

As we have seen, a couple of years ago I was truly honoured to visit Dumfries House, where I spent a wonderful afternoon talking about Thomas Chippendale while my host, Prince Charles, showed me around. I absolutely fell in love with a partner's desk in the library, which I'd suggest, if it were to be offered for sale, would attract interest at between £2 million and £3 million. I was in antique-furniture heaven, everything worked perfectly and the drawers all ran so superbly. All in all, the furniture was presented so wonderfully that it looked trapped in time, displayed in practically the same condition as the day it was made. This is partly because Dumfries House was used primarily during the summer and was shut up for most of the year, so there is very little fading, and temperatures were kept fairly constant, thus inhibiting warping and other damage. I'm drawn to conclude that a collection of eighteenth-century Thomas Chippendale furniture doesn't get much better than the one at Dumfries House, and it's available for you to view from March to October and, indeed, at advertised times throughout the winter months, too. If you get the opportunity to stand in awe as I did, I hope you too will appreciate the intelligent design and aesthetic beauty of Thomas's work displayed exactly as it was meant to be seen in this stunning setting. There are other fine examples of Chippendale at Petworth House, the Victoria and Albert, Syon House, Harewood House and West Wycombe Park, as well as many other collections around the British Isles. Go take a look for yourself to see exactly why I am so much in awe of Thomas Chippendale.

CHURCHILL'S LEGACY: A VISIT TO CHARTWELL MANOR

The Greatest Briton who ever lived? In a poll conducted for a BBC TV series, the British public voted that the Greatest Briton was Sir Winston Churchill, the man who led the nation through the dark years of the Second World War, defying Hitler even when Britain stood alone in Europe, facing the very real threat of invasion in 1940. His stalwart leadership during the war is what he is best remembered for, but when he gave his incredible speech in the House of Commons on 4 June 1940, in which he said, 'We shall fight on the beaches, we shall fight on the landing grounds, we shall fight in the fields and in the streets, we shall fight in the hills; we shall never surrender', it is easy to forget that he was already sixty-five years old – the age at which most of us would hope to be putting our feet up in retirement. Churchill had already lived an amazing life by then.

He was born at Blenheim in Oxfordshire, the ancestral home of his grandfather, the Duke of Marlborough on 30 November 1874. Churchill spent his early years at Blenheim, which was designed by Sir John Vanbrugh with the gardens laid out by Capability Brown, so it

is surely from here that Churchill developed his eye for art and his famously expensive tastes! Churchill went to Harrow School and, never having been the most diligent of students, on his second attempt he was accepted for officer training at the Royal Military Academy Sandhurst. He graduated in 1895, so as an officer he would have sworn allegiance to Queen Victoria, and he went on to serve in India, Sudan and, during the Second Boer War, South Africa. In Sudan in 1898, during the Battle of Omdurman, Churchill actually took part in the British Army's last ever cavalry charge. During most of this time, he was writing reports for magazines and newspapers as a war correspondent to supplement his income. Churchill's father inherited a courtesy title, but not a great fortune, and, although his mother came from a reasonably wealthy American family, Churchill always had to work hard to support the kind of lifestyle he led.

Even when he entered politics, which was not particularly well paid, Churchill relied on his writing to pay the bills, especially when he bought Chartwell House in 1922 for the princely sum of £5,000, which would be the

The beautiful surroundings of the Chartwell estate.

equivalent of about £270,000 today. He then spent around £18,000 on renovating and extending the building over the next two years. In 2014 I was lucky enough to be able to pay a visit to Chartwell while filming for the BBC, and I had the best possible guide when I was there: Sir Winston Churchill's granddaughter, Celia Sandys, who helped me to find out more about the man behind the V-sign.

I met Celia on the steps leading to the house. Her appearance was striking: cropped red hair and strong features – a very elegant and intelligent lady who is an author, lecturer and TV presenter, having written several books about her grandfather. We chatted in the rose garden that had been designed by Lady Clementine Churchill, doubtless a place of solace and artistic inspiration for the busy politician. Celia recalled the many happy summers she had spent at Chartwell during her younger years. She spent a lot of time with her grandfather in her late teens and recalled him as an affectionate family man.

'He didn't buy a house: he bought a view!' she told me as we surveyed the glorious landscape stretching endlessly beyond the house. 'He was brought up by his nanny, Mrs Everest, who came from Kent. She used to say that Kent was the garden of England, and I think she probably put that into his head.'

The view from Chartwell was stunning, with miles and miles of beautiful countryside stretching off into the Weald of Kent beyond an immaculate garden filled with an array of plants and flowers. Churchill was inspired by nature and the vistas, but he also wanted the house to be a place for his children. He loved spending time there with Clementine, their five children and their grandchildren, Chartwell serving as the family home from 1922 to 1965. During the war years, the house was infrequently visited, partly because Churchill was kept busy running the war and the country from London, and partly because it was rather too close to the coast. Had the Germans actually managed to invade and fight their way north from the coast into Kent, Churchill could possibly have viewed the battlegrounds from the windows of Chartwell!

and chairs designed by Heal's to Churchill's precise specification. There is still a Heal's store in Tottenham Court Road in London, but when this dining set was made in the 1920s Heal's was a family-owned business supplying bespoke furniture. The dining room has arched windows that let light, and the garden, flood into the space, and there is less wall area here to display Churchill's paintings than there is in other parts of the house.

The paintings were the first things that

Chartwell's dining room.

Today, the house looks much as it did during the 1950s, albeit that some of the rooms house exhibits displayed as they might be in a museum. In the dining room stand the table

struck me as I walked in. Churchill began painting at the age of forty, a late start for an artist, but he was certainly prolific. He had a natural talent for oil on canvas, creating

more than five hundred oil paintings within his lifetime and giving many away. President Roosevelt, President Truman and President Eisenhower were among the lucky, high-profile recipients, but the artwork was more to Churchill than just a way of showing his appreciation. Churchill's paintings, it seems, were a lifeline and he used them to help him shake off the so-called 'black dog' of depression that plagued him throughout his life. While

The Goldfish Pool at Chartwell.

it was his sister-in-law who first encouraged Churchill to take up painting, he was later given instruction by a friend, French artist Paul Lucien Maze, whom he met while they were both serving in the army during the First World War. He was also given a few tips by other artist friends such as Walter Sickert and Sir William Nicholson, and there is a fascinating collection of Churchill canvasses in his studio (separate from the main house) at Chartwell. Built in the 1930s, the walls of the studio are adorned with paintings, most of them unframed and many of them incomplete. There are paints and brushes scattered around the room and there is another partly finished canvas set on an easel beside the armchair in

which Churchill sat when he painted – it really is as though he just walked out the door.

Not long after I took a look round his studio, Sotheby's auctioned one of Churchill's paintings, *The Goldfish Pool at Chartwell*, with an estimate of £400,000 to £600,000. It sold for £1.8 million! But, though all of his works were impressive in their own right, there was one painting that I was particularly curious about: *Mary's First Speech*.

'Mary was the youngest child, born in 1922,' Celia explained as we strolled through the grounds. 'My grandfather wanted to do bricklaying, and he helped build a large part of these walls.' She indicated the red-brick walls that stood beside the house. 'He

decided to build a little house for Mary called the Marycot, and so he did a painting of her laying the foundation stone. It was the best form of therapy to relieve stress and one that he really enjoyed.'

And Celia was certain that one of her grandfather's greatest pleasures in life was to be surrounded by as many family members as possible.

'Chartwell meant everything to him,' she said. 'He always said that a day away from Chartwell was a day wasted. But at the same time he needed the adrenaline rush of travel.'

And travel he did. Anyone visiting Chartwell can see that Churchill's travels are reflected in his art. Paintings of mountains, beaches and mosques are nestled among the paintings of the house itself and the English countryside. Even the Egyptian pyramids have made their way into the collection. When he wasn't outside relaxing with a bit of bricklaying, Churchill was in his studio painting, and, when he wasn't in his studio, he was working in his study on the first floor of the main house.

As I walked into the study, I got the sense that this was yet another place that the man had never left. It looked to be exactly as he would have known it, so much so that any minute I half expected him to walk around the corner. On his desk were so many photos

of family members that there could hardly have been room to work, and everywhere I looked there were bookshelves lining the walls. The room is a good size; in fact, it feels a bit like a miniature version of a great hall in a baronial mansion with exposed ceiling beams, and that 'great hall' feeling is enhanced by the way that colourful banners are hung from those beams. These are not mere decorations but have historical significance of their own. One is Churchill's standard as the Lord Warden of the Cinque Ports, one is his standard as a Knight of the Garter and the third is a Union Flag given to Churchill by Lord Alexander of Tunis. This was the first Union Flag to fly over a liberated capital during the Second World War when it was raised in Rome on 5 June 1944.

But, in a room steeped in history, it is undoubtedly the desk that draws you like a magnet. It was here that Churchill wrote some of his greatest speeches. It was here that he started his four-volume work, *A History of the English-Speaking Peoples*, before the war and it was here that he wrote his six-volume history, *The Second World War*. Among his other works are a novel, two autobiographies and three volumes of memoirs, but there was much, much more. Over the course of his life, Churchill wrote an estimated eight to ten million words, in more than forty books, thousands of newspaper and magazine articles and at least two film scripts. He was awarded the Nobel Prize in Literature in 1953 'for his mastery of historical and biographical description as well as for brilliant oratory in

defending exalted human values'. Not bad for someone who was a bit of a duffer at school!

It should be remembered, however, that unlike painting – which was a labour of love – Churchill's written work provided him with his main source of income. It was his writing that paid for Chartwell House and allowed him the pleasure of having his family gathered around him. When he was a child, Churchill saw little of his parents. He was raised mainly by his nanny, Elizabeth Everest, who went into service with the Churchills in 1875. She was known as 'Mrs' Everest, even though she never married, as it was the custom to give nannies that title at the time. Churchill said in his autobiography that, 'Mrs Everest it was who looked after me and tended all my wants. It was to her that I poured out all my many troubles.' Having Chartwell as a family home meant that Churchill could have his children and grandchildren close to him. He didn't want them at arm's length as he had been with his parents.

'He was lovely,' reflected Celia, who was twenty-one years old when her grandfather died in 1965. 'For us he was just Grandpapa. After the war the only people who took Winston Churchill completely for granted were his grandchildren. Even his children were in awe of him.'

Chartwell House is now run by the National Trust, so you can take a look at the Churchill's bricklaying skills yourself. In fact, it has been owned by the National Trust for more than seventy years – even while Churchill was still living there. Before the war, in 1938, Churchill was struggling financially and came very close to selling the property. After the war, in 1946, he again faced a financial crisis. The cost of running the whole estate, which included farms that were operating at a loss, was crippling. Wealthy friends of Churchill made donations to the National Trust that allowed it to buy the property and then offer Churchill a fifty-year lease so that he could spend the rest of his days there. When Churchill died, Lady Churchill gave up the lease, returning Chartwell to the National Trust, which opened the house to the public in 1966.

As I thanked Celia for her time and walked away from the house and its grounds, I found myself deep in thought. The encounter had left me craving a piece of the great man's past, something that would bring me closer to all of the wonderful history I had experienced at Chartwell. Before I could even begin to think about how to achieve that, fate intervened. In the days after my meeting with Celia, as if by magic, a Sotheby's catalogue dropped through our letterbox, detailing an auction of items from the legacy of Churchill. This was

the sale of the contents of the late Baroness Mary Soames's Holland Park residence. Mary Soames was Churchill's youngest daughter – the Mary from the *Mary's First Speech* painting. It was also the same sale in which *The Goldfish Pool at Chartwell* went under the hammer for a king's ransom. There were other things that caught my eye, however, that looked as if they were more within my means. Provenance is key when it comes to an item's value, and, when a piece of artwork or furniture is connected to a specific person or date, that value increases dramatically.

As soon as I saw the catalogue I knew I had to own something from it, so the next day the family and I all sat around the breakfast table and discussed what would be best to buy. We settled upon a modest purchase: a nineteenth-century bookcase of varnished and ebonised pine. Its estimated value was set at £250 to £400. This was much more my price range and it would be a marvellous addition to the Martin household, perfect for Dylan's bedroom to house his collection of fossils and shells. What a talking point!

I thought I would go in punchy, with a strong £1,000-to-£1,200 maximum bid, as that would definitely secure it, seeing off anyone else. I could almost hear, in my head, Edward Elgar's 'Land of Hope and Glory' playing, and I thought to myself, 'Britain expects every man to do his duty.' So, when the day of the auction came, off I went to Bond Street. The bookcase quickly reached its lower estimate and the bids kept rolling in. This was OK. I hadn't really expected bidding to stop at £250, but still the figure rose, and the tension with it. I watched in dismay as the price shot wildly upwards, exceeding £400, then £500, then even £1,000. It seemed unreal. The bidding rose to over £2,000 but I had pulled out long before then. Still the bids kept going, reaching £2,500, then £3,000 and finally closing at a staggering £4,000.

I was in shock. I felt stupid. I couldn't believe the amount by which I'd misjudged the bookcase's value. But then, I reasoned, so had the Sotheby's catalogue, and I suppose that is exactly what this story goes to show. The perceived value of an item is in the eye of the beholder, and my experience serves as a reminder that with any antique, particularly one chosen by someone as hugely admired as Churchill, you can never really put a monetary value on history.

The power of Churchill's legacy ensured that the lots were all taken to their estimates and beyond, busting levels, giving Sotheby's a total hammer price of £12.8 million for the sale, with around a 25 per cent buyers' premium and a 25 per cent sellers' commission. That's a nice day's work!

Meet the Experts: James Lewis

James Lewis is one of the most recognisable faces of the antiques world. He started his career in London before moving to the Midlands, where he is now CEO of a leading auction house, Bamfords of Derby. During his time as an auctioneer he has won Auctioneer of the Year, awarded by his fellow professionals, as well as setting the world record for the longest solo auction of twenty-six hours for charity. His skills as an auctioneer have seen him travel to Los Angeles, Monaco and Paris and throughout Africa. He has hosted events for several A-list celebrities and international organisations.

In the world of antiques he loves the unusual and has a special interest in tribal art, Derby porcelain, sculpture and fine furniture. James's other passion, earning him the nickname Lionheart, is his love of animals and wildlife. He has been a major fundraiser and patron for the Born Free Foundation for almost twenty years.

'I love the auction room, an environment where the most unlikely fellows can find themselves together, hooked and drawn in by a common passion for history, culture, art and antiques or simply the possibility of finding that last piece to complete or add to a collection.

'Antiques for me are a portal into another world, another civilisation, or simply another period in time. They are the closest thing we will ever have to time travel. Holding an object that can have been acquired for a few pounds, but that was made and used two thousand or more years ago, can give us clues to life in a different world. Bundles of Roman coins, ancient Egyptian scarabs or Greek pottery vessels made, owned and used at the time of Christ can be the most underrated and best value objects at auction.

'For the last fifteen years I have regularly carried Roman coins to give to children who like antiques and to encourage their interest, and, although only worth a few pounds, they certainly stimulate their imagination and curiosity. One of the favourite objects in my collection is a large Roman brass ladle unearthed in the excavations at Pompeii in 1760. We have all read Pliny the Younger's writings of the disaster and devastation of Pompeii on 24 August AD 79, when Vesuvius erupted and covered the town in hot ash. It is this that makes the ladle exciting, the history, the age, who used it and knowing that it lay there undiscovered for 1,700 years. The ladle could have been used in the many street-side takeaway restaurants that were a major part of life 2,000 years ago throughout Roman Italy. Anyone who thinks that the take-

A miniature nineteenth-century book, Bijou Picture of London, which was auctioned at Bamfords.

away is a twentieth-century invention could not be more wrong as some estimate up to 80 per cent of meals were taken out at that time.

'One of my favourite auctions at Bamfords was the sale of a wooden trunk and contents owned by a sailor, Edward McKenzie. McKenzie was no ordinary seaman. He and the trunk had accompanied Scott of the Antarctic on one of the most famous adventures of all time. The

trunk contained objects from the 1912 Scott expedition, the most noteworthy of which was a leather jotter that detailed his journey. The jotter details how McKenzie left Derbyshire and arrived at Cardiff station with his several oilskin bags. It tells how the station master gave him a compass for his journey, and there in the trunk was the compass. It then details the journey to South Africa, picking up Scott, then to Australia, New Zealand and finally the South Pole, where Amundsen's ship, the Fram, was already moored. Scott decided to moor 100 metres to the south of them, thereby placing them closer to the South Pole, and, on leaving the gangplank, gave the appropriate gesture.

'Many days were taken on the icefields setting up camp, doing research, while the world-famous photographer, Herbert Ponting, took photographs. A selection of these photographs remained in the trunk. McKenzie writes how on one occasion Ponting was attacked by a killer whale, which beached itself on the ice in the attack. The trunk also contained cutlery, carvings and other fascinating objects relating to the expedition. The jotter finally detailed the realisation that Scott and his fellow adventurers had been killed on the journey. The sale attracted bids from all over the world from famous explorers, museums and collectors. Many pieces were bought by the Cambridge Research Institute, who already had McKenzie's polar clothing in their collection. The money raised from the sale was life-changing for the owner.

'There is a significant difference between a buyer furnishing a home or buying individual objects they like, and a collector. A collector can be obsessive, it can be all encompassing if you have an addictive personality – beware of becoming a collector. I started collecting at the age of fifteen. I wish somebody had given me that advice. Thirty years later I have an obsession with snuff boxes. The strange thing about collecting is that you end up buying examples for your collection that you don't even like simply to fill a gap to make your collection complete.

'Anyone considering involving themselves in the world of antiques and auctions will never find a more fascinating, diverse and wonderful world and, whether you have an object worth just a few pounds or hundreds of thousands of pounds is irrelevant. Get out to the antique fairs and the auctions and have a wonderful time!'

Meet the Experts: Philip Serrell

'In November of 1999 BBC Bristol called me and asked me if I wanted to appear in a new programme called *Bargain Hunt*. I ummed and ahhed for a while and eventually agreed. It was a decision I've never looked back from and, more importantly, enjoyed every minute of. Then, not long after, I was sitting in my saleroom and someone from the BBC telephoned again and said, "We're going to make this new programme called *Flog It!* and wondered whether you wanted to record the first show for us." Well, I thought about it for a nanosecond and replied in the affirmative.

'Off we went to Stow-on-the-Wold and about thirty-five people appeared to have their priceless heirlooms valued. The day was, without doubt, a learning curve and we are today where we are with *Flog It!* Many would argue that the show has become something of a national institution as valuation days produce queues that stretch to the horizon and the opinion of me and my fellow experts counts for nowt as the reality of the auction room mixes disappointment with elation.

'Over the years I think we all develop a television persona and mine seems to be that of the grumpy old auctioneer, which has resulted in my being typecast on further programmes such as *Put Your Money Where Your Mouth Is* and *The Antiques Road Trip*. I have to say it's been a fantastic journey and friendships that have developed with Paul and my fellow experts have been long-lasting and important parts of my life. Just a little snippet of a television secret that I ought to divulge: I'm not really that grumpy, I've just got one of those faces!

'As well as being in front of the camera on valuation days I've also been lucky enough to have had *Flog It!* in my saleroom for auction days. These days are always exciting but when the cameras are in the saleroom the level does rise a few notches. In March 2011 the excitement level reached the top of the ladder as far as I was concerned. The BBC appeared in Malvern to film and brought with them a painting by the wonderfully named Sir John Alfred Arnesby Brown. Sir John, who was born in 1866 and lived to the ripe old age of eighty-eight, was regarded by many as one of Britain's greatest twentieth-century landscape painters. He was elected to the Royal Academy in 1903 and this painting was not only a prime example of his work but also completely flavour of the month in terms of desirability. It had been estimated to realise between £4,000 and £6,000 on the valuation day but this was cast to the winds by Internet, telephone and bidders in the room as it sold for £10,500 – a real *Flog It!* moment!

'I've been lucky enough through the medium of television to share with many my love of porcelain produced in my home city of Worcester. That has resulted in Worcester porcelain being shipped for sale to my Worcestershire saleroom from as far afield as the United States of America. I think my interest was fired by a school trip around the museum, where the curator, a certain Henry Sandon, brought the contents of the cabinets to life for me. In 2009, this connection was completed when I was asked to sell an urn painted by the great Harry Davis.

HORSES THROUGH HISTORY

I have always admired horses. They are amazing animals, incredibly powerful, utterly beautiful, remarkably intelligent and often endearingly affectionate. Their strength, their agility, their speed and yet their surprising gentleness are a constant source of wonder. We, especially in Britain, may think that the dog is man's best friend, but the horse trumps the dog in so many ways, although I wouldn't want ours sleeping at the bottom of our bed!

At home we have a 16.1hh Thoroughbred called Frankie. For anyone not familiar with the way that horses are measured, 'hh' stands for 'hands high'. It's good to know a bit about what this means because the term crops up all the time when equestrian antiques are being discussed, not least when you are looking at a painting of a famous horse. So what does it actually mean? Well, the 'hand' measurement has been used since the time of the ancient Egyptians and beyond. It was taken to be the breadth of a male hand, or the height of a clenched fist. Obviously, that is a pretty rough measurement because a big bloke like Arnold Schwarzenegger is going to have far larger hands than a smaller chap like Danny DeVito, so in England in 1540,

good old King Henry VIII decreed that the size of the 'hand' measurement should be standardised to 4 inches (10cm). That means that, at 16.1hh, Frankie is 65 inches (162.5cm), because 16.1hh means 16 hands and one inch.

Horses are measured not to the top of their heads but to the withers, which is the point on the back between the shoulder blades, roughly where the neck could be said to join the back. The average Thoroughbred is 16 hands (making Frankie just about right) and ponies are up to 14.2 hands.

Frankie was actually bred and trained as a racehorse, but has very much settled into life as part of our family, which is amazing when you consider what would have been required of her in her previous life – the training, exercise and running at full pelt with a jockey on her back. A racehorse in full gallop is a sight to behold, able to take up to 150 strides a minute with each stride averaging at least 20 feet, so a Thoroughbred can reach speeds of more than 40 mph. And this is not the meandering, civilised 40 mph you would do tootling down a country lane in a car – on the back of a horse 40mph is a very different experience. You can feel

During WWII, the Germans used thousands of horses to pull supply wagons.

the wind against your face, feel the horse's muscles powering it forward, hear the hooves pounding the ground beneath you and feel your own muscles straining as you work to keep yourself in balance with your equine partner. And then there's the adrenaline rush, the thrill and the joy of communicating at speed with a real live animal that has a mind of its own. You certainly don't get that from a leisurely car drive in the countryside.

Horse racing is today's biggest money maker in terms of equestrianism, but this wasn't always the case. A century ago, there were more horses on our streets than there were cars, trucks and buses. Horses were our main form of transport and even as late as the Second World War, when we were previously discussing Churchill defying the Germans to invade Britain, the German invasion force would have included thousands of horses to pull supply wagons. Horses have been fundamental to human progress – indispensable to farmers for pulling ploughs and carts. It is no coincidence that the term 'horsepower' is used to describe the rate at which an engine works. Equines have journeyed with us as partners through thousands of years, taking us from our first steps towards civilisation all the way through the Industrial Revolution.

Yet the peacetime role of these gentle creatures – vegetarians who do not kill to feed – is perhaps eclipsed by the way that they have been used in war. For Britain, the horses of war have been fundamental to our history. One glimpse of a squadron of the Queen's Household Cavalry at the Trooping the Colour ceremony or any other royal pageant shows how awesome the massed regiments of mounted soldiers must have looked when going into battle.

Some time ago I filmed an episode of *Flog It!* where we took a look at memorabilia from the Crimean War, and this involved a trip to the National Army Museum in Chelsea, London, next door to the Royal Hospital Chelsea, home to the 'Chelsea Pensioners' retired service personnel. Unlike the Royal Hospital, however, which is more than 300 years old, The National Army Museum was opened in 1971, although it was built on the site of an old Royal Hospital infirmary. Having recently undergone a £23.7 million

The Household Cavalry Mounted Regiment.

refurbishment, the museum has five galleries of displays on British military history from the modern era right back to the English Civil War in 1642.

It was in the museum that I saw the skeleton of a horse, Marengo, standing in all its glory – albeit minus two hooves. I was fascinated by it, so much so that after filming had finished I returned to the museum with my son, Dylan. I had been fascinated by the Napoleonic wars since the age of thirteen, which had led me to join modelling societies and even to embark on a trip to Waterloo in my teens, so it was only natural that seeing the skeleton got me thinking about the story that unfolded while the horse was still alive – and of course, about his famous owner.

Napoleon Bonaparte, perhaps the most famous Frenchman who ever lived, actually had Italian parents. Napoleon was born in Ajaccio on the island of Corsica in 1769, the year that Corsica became part of France rather than part of Italy. As a child, Napoleon spoke Corsican and Italian – he didn't learn French until he was ten years old. He came from quite a wealthy family and his father was a lawyer who represented Corsica at the court of France's King Louis XVI. Napoleon went to school and military college in France, becoming an officer in the French Army, but actually fought against France

as a Corsican nationalist in the early years of the French Revolution. Napoleon rose swiftly through the ranks in the army and by the time the revolution was over in 1799, he was a general. By 1804, he had outflanked France's floundering politicians to become Emperor of France and the following year he also became King of Italy. He was to remain in power as Emperor until 1814.

He led several successful campaigns during the revolutionary wars and his innovation, charisma and limitless ambition won not only the hearts of the French but also 53 out of the 60 battles he fought, which in turn allowed for a huge expansion of the French empire. But though he was brave and tireless on horseback, Napoleon's seat in the saddle was poor and Marengo became a lifeline as his mount, disguising and accommodating the great leader's lack of equestrian skill. He carried Napoleon safely through the Battle of Marengo, after which he was named, and subsequently completed fifteen years of service, himself being wounded eight times and narrowly avoiding capture more than once. But like his owner, despite his achievements, Marengo was conspicuously lacking in height. Napoleon was about 5ft 7in tall (1.7m), which was actually slightly above average for a Frenchman at that time, and Marengo stood at 14hh –

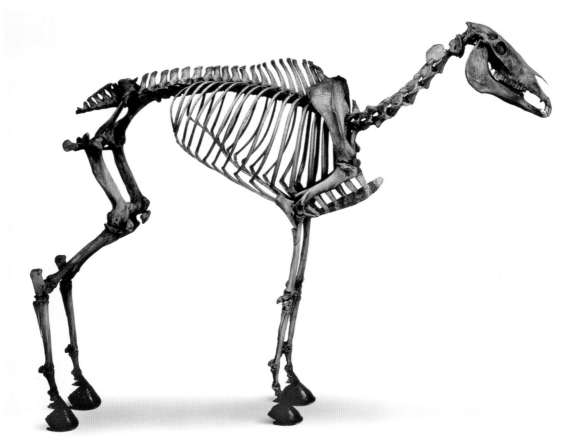

The skeleton of Napoleon's horse Marengo, on display in the National Army Museum.

a pony by today's standards and not at all the typical dimensions of a warhorse. Yet it was this that made him a perfect fit for the diminutive Napoleon. Together, Napoleon and Marengo led the charge through the Napoleonic Wars, fighting in the Battle of Austerlitz, the Battle of Jena–Auerstedt, the Battle of Wagram and finally the Battle of Waterloo in 1815, where Napoleon was defeated and Marengo was captured.

Widely acknowledged as being the driving force in securing Napoleon's defeat, the Duke of Wellington has become known as Napoleon's nemesis. Born in Dublin to an aristocratic Irish family, Arthur Wesley (the family name was later changed to Wellesley) went to school at Eton and, like Napoleon, also attended a military college in France. He served as an officer with the British Army in Flanders in 1794 and was posted to India in 1796. Wellington fought many battles in India, returning to Europe in 1805

'Napoleon on His Favourite Charger, Marengo' by James Edwin McConnell.

as a Major-General and with a knighthood. He became a Member of Parliament and seemed set for high political office, but within three years he was recalled to the military to fight in Portugal against the armies of Napoleon. He fought Napoleon's army in Spain in 1808, and between 1808 and 1814, when Napoleon's power was at its peak, he became allies with the Portuguese and Spanish in order to force France to withdraw from the Spanish peninsula. His victories led to him being made Duke of Wellington, amongst a host of other honours and titles. It was also during this time that he met his own battle partner, his horse, the great Copenhagen. Standing at

'The Duke of Wellington and His Charger Copenhagen' by David Wilkie.

can be drawn between the two, and it would appear that these two deadly enemies held a good degree of admiration for each other. Napoleon approved of Wellington's caution and courage and Wellington admired Napoleon's skills as a strategic planner. A visit to Apsley House, the home of the duke and his descendants, whilst filming an episode of *Flog It!* allowed me to experience this admiration first-hand. Approaching the house is a strangely unnerving experience because, standing on the other side of the road looking across at the front of the building, is a statue of the Duke of Wellington mounted on Copenhagen and guarded by four infantrymen, all cast in bronze made from guns captured at Waterloo!

The house itself was built by Robert Adam in the 1770s for Lord Apsley, who was then Lord Chancellor, and was originally a red brick mansion. Wellington's elder brother bought it in 1807 but sold it to Wellington ten years later when the duke needed a grand house in London as he became more involved in politics – he became Prime Minister in 1828. Two years after buying the house, Wellington greatly extended the building and when he became Prime Minister he transformed its appearance completely by having it clad in

just 15hh, with Arabian and Thoroughbred bloodlines, Copenhagen was named in honour of the British victory at the Second Battle of Copenhagen (where Wellington had commanded an infantry brigade) and had a career similar to Marengo. He was the duke's mount during the Battle of Waterloo and as a result, went down in history.

When you consider the way that their lives developed, it seems almost inevitable that the paths of the Duke of Wellington and Napoleon would cross. Striking similarities

Bath stone. But it is not the house itself, or even its French-inspired, hugely impressive interiors that are evidence of Wellington's respect for Napoleon. For that you need look no further than the bottom of the curving staircase in the entrance hall where stands a statue of Napoleon, placed there at the command of the duke himself. He may, of course, have found the statue a bit of a giggle. It is a superb example of the work of the talented Italian sculptor Antonio Canova and undoubtedly looks like Napoleon, although it is 11ft 4in (3.45m) tall, which

Napoleon was not; it has the musculature and proportions of a great athlete, which Napoleon was not; and it is nude with only a fig leaf covering his modesty! The statue is titled *Napoleon as Mars the Peacemaker* and was commissioned by Napoleon for display in The Louvre, but when he saw the finished article, even he decided that it looked too athletic and banned it from ever going on display. It was looted by the British as 'spoils of war' after the Battle of Waterloo.

Canova's work was very fashionable in nineteenth-century Britain, so the Duke of Wellington would have been pleased to have the statue, especially as he had a personal connection with the subject. Napoleon and Wellington were alike in many ways. Both were born in 1769. Both were born to aristocratic families whose heritage was different to those of the countries for which they later fought. Both saw swift and steady promotion through the ranks in military, even though both were seen as unremarkable in their youth. Both became leaders of their countries and, of course, both placed immense value on their horses.

Copenhagen ended his days a hero, with the duke continuing to ride him in parades and other ceremonial events after Waterloo. The horse was then retired to the duke's country estate at Stratfield Saye House in

The imposing statue of the Duke of Wellington, near Apsley House.

'Napoleon as Mars the Peacemaker' by Antonio Canova – note Napoleon's almost comically exaggerated musculature, which probably amused Wellington no end!

Hampshire, where he lived out his days. After Copenhagen's burial, the Duke of Wellington was asked to disinter his horse so he could be exhibited at the United Services Institution museum alongside Marengo, but he firmly refused. Before the horse's burial, however, one of Copenhagen's hooves was removed by one of Wellington's servants, which went very much against the Duke's wishes. The Duke was away at the time of Copenhagen's death, but an unexpected return in order to see the horse buried allowed him to catch sight of the missing hoof. His rage was so fearful at the time that no one dared to tell him how it had happened, but the mystery was eventually unravelled. After Wellington's death some thirty years later, the servant, now elderly, returned the hoof to the second duke and finally offered an explanation. The hoof was made into an ink-stand and still resides at Stratfield Saye House today.

And what of Marengo? After the Battle of Waterloo, the stallion was captured by William Henry Francis Petre, who brought him back to the United Kingdom and sold him on to Lieutenant-Colonel Angerstein of the Grenadier Guards. Marengo then stood at stud until the age of twenty-seven, finally dying at the age of thirty-eight. He outlived Napoleon, who had died a full ten years before. After his death, his skeleton was preserved and displayed at the United Services Institution museum before being passed to the National Army Museum, where I witnessed it first-hand. His missing two hooves had been made into ornaments; one used as a snuff box and given to the officers of the Brigade of Guards, and the other made into a silver inkwell and kept for generations by the Angerstein family. The inkwell is now on loan to the Household Cavalry Museum, where it is kept on display. Marengo's skeleton was recently cleaned and restored by experts from the Natural History Museum before going back on display at the Army Museum along with uniforms and artefacts belonging to Napoleon and the Duke of Wellington.

Antiques and artefacts from the Napoleonic wars is a very collectible field, as is equestrian memorabilia. Artwork featuring horses is more strongly contested at auction than depictions of any other animal, so it comes as no surprise that when it involves the famous horses and equestrians of history, the value of a piece of art skyrockets. As well as collectibles making great furnishing pieces, equine art features some of the biggest names in the art world. Names such as Alfred Munnings and George Stubbs grace the corners of highly sought-after paintings, all of which have horses as their subjects.

Stubbs was best known for mastering the scenery beyond the awkward space between the horse's front and hind legs, so often left out in paintings by other artists, and he was even rumoured to have transposed his horses onto more interesting backgrounds. Ironically though, his most famous work was arguably *Whistlejacket*, which saw him pay particular attention to the details of the horse's appearance, but neglect to include any background at all. Although some may immediately think of Stubbs when it comes to paintings of horses, Munnings is every bit as famous. He attempted to join the army during the First World War but was deemed unfit for service. Instead, he made a name for himself as a war artist and created works such as *The Red Prince Mare*. This incredible painting sold for a whopping $7,848,000 at auction in 2007, which was a record breaker for the Munnings collection.

Napoleon, Wellington, Marengo and

Sir Alfred Munnings at work on his opus, 'The Red Prince Mare'.

Copenhagen are now long gone, but their stories are kept alive by the artefacts, ephemera and works of art displayed at places like the National Army Museum and Apsley House (which is now run by English Heritage and open to the public), so why not go and take a look at Marengo's skeleton and the statue that Napoleon never wanted you to see? Artworks and relics like these provide us with a window to the past and, as it happens, a similar equine skeleton to Marengo is set up amongst the antiques at my home, though of course it is not nearly so famous. The skeleton is ordinary, standing at just over 14.2hh which puts it precisely between the heights of Marengo and Copenhagen. It is only just over height for a pony, but far from that making it less impressive, I actually see it as all the more inspiring. Recalling those great horses from history, the skeleton serves as a reminder not only of the past, but of the fact that even the unlikeliest among us can achieve great things.

Aspley House.

George Stubbs'
'Whistlejacket', the king
of equestrian art.

ETHNOGRAPHICA

The word 'ethnography' is all about the study of people and cultures, which sounds a bit more of a scientific subject than you might think we are used to in the antiques game, but don't let that mislead you: there is plenty of science, study and analysis involved in antiques. Ethnographica, obviously related to ethnography, basically refers to collections of artefacts of cultural significance from different ethnic groups around the world. Sometimes referred to as 'tribal art', this genre of antique collecting acknowledges and celebrates the identities of the makers and often involves wonderfully artistic, creative pieces that exude a primal beauty.

From the earliest days of social interaction between cultures, goods that were traded included anything from animal skins to flints, beads, tools and religious artefacts. This trade spread fashions and designs, the influences of other cultures taking root far from the area, country or continent where the trade goods originated. The synergy of humanity, adopting the styles and identifiers of other cultures, is what makes the world such a truly vibrant, curious and wonderful place, where every civilisation has its own story and an identity that draws the admiration of others who are absorbed by new, unique designs and artistry.

The expansion of the British Empire from the late sixteenth century to its zenith in the early years of the twentieth – regardless of how we might nowadays debate the pros and cons of its political correctness – brought British culture and traditions to foreign domains and, just as the earliest traders influenced one another's ideas, it introduced the British to foreign cultures steeped in their own history. Everyone, whether missionary, merchant, politician, soldier or sailor, eagerly collected trophies for family and friends to gaze at in awe when they returned home. Imagine, this is the pre-camera and pre-mass-communication era. Other than these artefacts, only the drawings and paintings of generally amateur hands existed to show the general population and academics the sorts of things created by other cultures.

The mass appeal of ethnographica started in the nineteenth century, with a resurgence of interest in the 1930s and then again, most importantly, during the 1960s, when the hippy lifestyle and counterculture embraced a more simplistic world. Pop stars and starlets eagerly collected masks

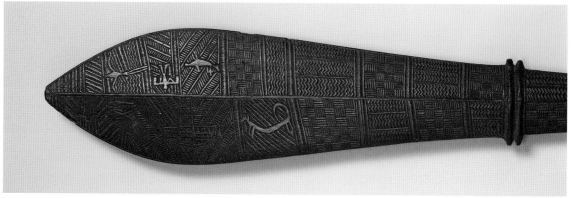

A Polynesian war club carved using a shark tooth.

and fetishes, beads, a myriad carvings and treen artefacts that shouted 'ethnographica', exuding a pagan artistry like nothing else. Each item had an aura, yet the simple way of explaining these items is to say they had the wow factor. And that's WOW! In big bold capital letters. At the same time, it's fair to say there was still a lot of post-colonial snobbery about ethnographica, simply because it was unsophisticated, lacking the perfect squares and neoclassical workmanship of mainstream antiques.

Today, some examples of ethnographic items make thousands of pounds in top auction houses such as Christie's, Sotheby's and Bonhams. South Pacific war clubs are very popular, often carved with identifiers of the number of kills it has made – animals, dots and squiggles, geometric patterns and, yes, even images of humans. In June 2015, at the Wallis & Wallis auction rooms, a

Tongan war club sold to a German collector for £16,500, while in August another Tongan example of just over 80cm sold for £16,000 plus 20 per cent buyer's premium, which is the charge levied by the auction house to make its money on items sold.

Back in December 2012, *Flog It!* made headlines for all the right reasons when a small collection of ethnographic items went under the hammer at Golding Young & Mawer auctions in Lincolnshire. Bringing these remarkable curios along to a *Flog It!* valuation day, no one, including me, the owners and, indeed, our experts, had an inkling about what would happen at auction. For owner Anne Bromley from Cleethorpes, silver expert Michael Baggott's on-the-day guide price of £200–£400, with a sensible reserve of £150, had already put a smile on her face. She was looking forward to the excitement of attending a *Flog It!* auction day with her eleven-year-old grandson Lewis, but nothing could prepare anyone for the incredible bidding frenzy that followed, or the dramatic moment when the hammer went down.

During the show, I'd abseiled inside Lincoln Cathedral and I'd picked raspberries as I pottered around the gardens of another fabulous location, Normanby Hall, a stunning Regency mansion designed by Robert Smirke and built in 1825. Once owned by the Dukes of Buckingham, original owners of Buckingham Palace, Normanby Hall made a wonderful setting for what became one of *Flog It!*'s most amazing tales when Anne's ethnographica was to reach truly regal heights! Unlike with the raspberries, there was no sour taste, just Wow! Wow! Wow!

Many of our valuation days uncover treasures once forgotten in wardrobes, and people bring them along for our experts to pick over. Anne was no exception. She'd been given a small collection of items – spears, shields, an axe and a bottle gourd – as a gift and, concerned about the spears hurting her young grandchildren, she'd put them at the back of the cupboard until one day she was having a clearout and thought *'Flog It!? I know: maybe they're worth a few quid.'* She needed some money to renovate her dining room, so jumped in the car with a collection of artefacts and drove along the A180 to our valuation day.

Michael's opening comment – 'Anne, you don't look like a lady to be messed with' – raised a chuckle, as Anne presented her weapons and told her story. She thought they were African and Michael went on to split the items into two categories: what he thought were true ethnographic items and what he considered to be tourist items, made to be sold as souvenirs rather than to be used for their apparent purpose. Words such as 'functionality' flowed from Michael's lips as he described something that he is so right in saying you should look out for in all antiques: colour! The muck and grease that had accumulated on the artefacts through years of human hands touching them might seem gross, but this is exactly what gives a functional item something commonly referred to as patina. Michael also picked up on the fact that the functional items lacked carving. They weren't too elaborate; they were tools, not ornaments.

There were two short fighting spears, a throwing axe, two shields and a calabash bottle gourd, which was probably African. As the name suggests, these bottles are made from a gourd that is the fruit of the calabash tree. They grow sub-tropically in Africa, Asia and South America and there have been excavated examples of these ingenious bottles dating back 13,000 years. Michael was right in saying that dating 'this stuff' is hard, even for an expert. He thought the collection dated from 1890 to 1900 but he did pick out the shields and the calabash as being the nicest items of the collection to him. I think everyone agreed that, irrespective of value, they would make an impressive wall display, but where to put them? And maybe Anne was right: I've two young children and weapons such as these would certainly draw their curiosity. Keeping them out of harm's

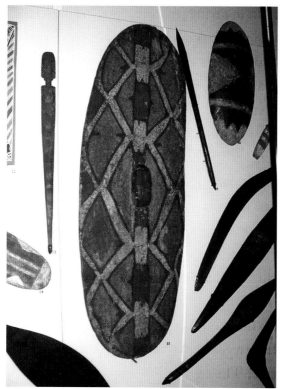

An Australian Aboriginal war shield.

way seemed the most sensible solution to her and I can see why.

Let me reiterate this. Yes, I know I've already told you, but did you take this in? Michael had valued them at £200 to £400 and Anne was utterly delighted. He wasn't going to spoil her dining-room dreams and so put a modest reserve of £150 on the collection, adding basically that the auction room would decide what they were worth.

In the modern world of Internet browsing, most auctions catalogue their sales online and it was as a result of this that an eagle-eyed museum curator from Sydney's Primitive Art Museum spotted the items while browsing and immediately identified an Aboriginal broad shield and a corroboree spear as exceptionally rare artefacts of huge significance to Australian heritage. A corroboree is a ceremonial meeting of Aborigines during which they interact with 'Dreamtime' using body paint, interpretative dance, music and costume to explore mythical tribal stories while sharing spiritual journeys among the tribe. Within the corroboree ceremony, the spear, unbeknown to anyone at the auction, held real significance.

Not realising the cultural significance of the items made what followed one of the most extraordinary *Flog It!* sales ever and undoubtedly one of the most memorable school holidays Lewis will ever remember. We were standing in the auction room, where tensions were already running high over whether Anne would be able to cover her dining-room decorating costs, but then it started to feel as if something really big was about to happen as, intriguingly, there were several booked phone lines. Clearly, there was interest from far afield. Bidding started at £500 and Anne was elated: her dining room was going to look pretty snazzy. But wait! There were bids galore coming in thick and fast! As bidding began to rise, you could have cut the atmosphere with a knife. The price climbed quickly into the thousands. A Sydney gallery bid frantically against the Museum of Primitive Art with neither party aware of the other's credentials. Anne and Lewis were truly speechless and Colin, the auctioneer, thought every time that he was hearing the final bid, but the bids rocketed to £3,200, £3,400 on the phone. At £5,800 I thought, 'Wow! Surely that's it.' Then £7,000 – Anne and Lewis were laughing. The ladies taking the calls were all nodding away. Up and up and up: £17,000, £18,000, £19,000 … 'Lot 145 at £30,000, at £30,000, going once, going twice, your last chance on the Internet, sold, £30,000!'

I think Anne's dining room is going to look like the Ritz!

Let me repeat that: £30,000 plus buyer's premium, thus securing the future of these enigmatic gems of Aboriginal culture for generations of Australians to come. Poor Michael cringes to this day whenever the items are mentioned! He is such a nice, genuine chap and one of Britain's top silver experts, and I have to say that he's taken all of the teasing soundly on the chin like the warm-hearted gentleman he truly is. In fairness to Michael, no one had an inkling that this lot would go sky high in the manner that it did. It even earned *Flog It!* a spot on the TV news! In the Manchester television studio no one could believe what had happened, but two people in Australia knew exactly what they were looking at and, accordingly, knew exactly the sum of money they were prepared to pay. When all's said and done, it just shows that knowledge of your subject is a powerful thing, and who's to say that one day soon we won't be valuing another incredible piece, perhaps picked up at a boot fair for just a few pounds by someone inspired by Anne and Lewis's amazing day.

After the sale and having realised the true significance of the items she would have gladly sold for a couple of hundred pounds, Anne expressed her genuine delight that these artefacts were finally going home. This really was an Indiana Jones moment for everyone at the auction and, indeed, the viewers at home. Sometimes a piece is so significant it deserves to be 'owned by the public' in the sense that it's displayed in a museum or sent home, where the descendants of its original creators can best appreciate it. There will always, of course, be a vast number of artefacts available to collect, treasured as they are for the beauty and craftsmanship that has earned them their place in contemporary salerooms alongside Chippendale chairs and Liberty mirrors as very saleable items. Indeed, as with English vernacular furniture, tribal art has its own regional identity, even over small geographic areas.

My tips for investment start inevitably with clubs and shields, but just as collectible are masks and spears. Focus on anything Polynesian or from the greater South Pacific and anything ethnographic from Australia and New Zealand should be considered, too. Prices are truly on the ascendency. Inuit carved animals, available for £100-plus, are worth investigation, too. Making a connection with something you buy for its beauty is hugely important, so, as ever, buy only things you like and then buy the best you can afford. Most items found at boot fairs and in jumble sales are likely to be post-1970s copies – not out-and-out forgeries at all, simply tourist pieces. Nevertheless, keep your eye out because you never know who might be getting rid of some period pieces they simply don't appreciate or understand. I can't emphasise this enough: knowledge is king! Visit the great collections and museums, seek out dealers who specialise and, above all, enjoy what you collect. The next time you glance at that boomerang your auntie sent over from Australia, look at it again: it might just be older than you think and worth considerably more, too!

Now *Flog It!* is all about the stories that surround items and the way our experts turn what might sometimes seem a dull item in the minds of the vendor into a little gem that might fund a holiday or, at least, a romantic dinner for two. Poor Michael apologised for getting Anne's valuation wrong, but he really wasn't to know – you can't be an expert in everything! It was a shock for Anne and a shock for all of us at the auction. Even Colin the auctioneer was shocked. We visited Anne a few days later in her pretty cottage. She was quick to say that, on the day of the auction, she felt as though she were not actually there. It was the strangest feeling she'd ever had in her life, like some kind of a dream where she couldn't see anybody. It was almost as though the auction gave Anne an out-of-body experience! Anne finished by suggesting everyone should check the back of

A traditional war club made from antler by the Haida people, from what is now northern British Columbia in Canada.

the wardrobe for hidden treasures!

Here's a tip, too, if you are interested in learning more about Aboriginal artefacts. What sets them apart is that African, Indian and Maori artefacts were traditionally carved with a knife. Aboriginal work is predominantly carved with a stone and this is why the grooves are more rounded. The stone will erode as it's rubbed into the wood and, when the maker is happy with the grooves, oil pigments are used to colour items.

Fijian throwing clubs look simply stunning and are, as you would expect, clubs that were thrown. With a long handle and carved bulbous end, these wonderful items currently start in salerooms at around £250,

with exquisite examples making much, much more. There are around thirty different types of club, most around 40cm in length. These clubs are known as 'Ula' and commonly exhibit a round end about the size of a grapefruit. Some have a naturalistic beauty, as they are made out of root clumps and known indigenously as 'I Ula Kobo', while others known as 'Kia Kava' bare striking similarities to Irish shillelaghs. A Fijian 'Totokia', or pineapple club, made in excess of £2,000 at auction in 2012. Fiji underwent years of tribal unrest, with many tribes indulging in ritual cannibalism, and the pineapple club was so named because its crown is full of nodules, making it look very like a pineapple. The

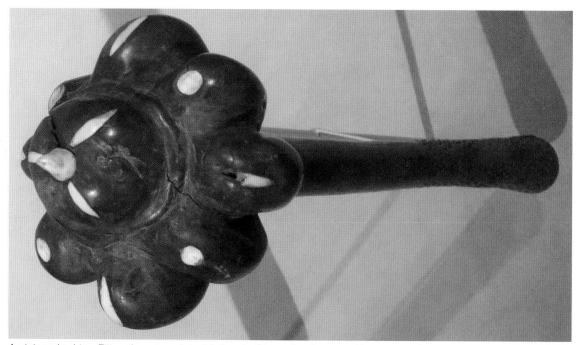

A vicious-looking Fijian throwing club. It is inset with marine ivory and human teeth.

nodules were designed to crack the skull. This might all sound quite horrific but, thinking back to my childhood, I realise I spent many hours in places such as the Tower of London looking at medieval weaponry, admired today for its craftsmanship and artistic beauty but actually brutal, functional, savage tools of war. Personally, I view these items in exactly the same way as ethnographic weapons: however gruesome their past, they remain tactile works of art.

Paddles from war canoes are heavily ebonised and, as such, fetch less than the other artefacts in general. As I write this there is one listed on a popular online auction site for just over £150.

I've literally skimmed the surface with a few choice tips, but there are a myriad items in which you can specialise. If you immerse yourself in the culture and find yourself lucky enough to visit a tribal location, please, please, please remember that you may need a permit or indeed be banned from removing any historic artefact at all from the country you are in. There are often stiff penalties for those who ignore the laws. I'm not saying you shouldn't look into importing something if the opportunity arises, just ensure you take

A truly stunning example of carved ivory art from West Africa. Dated between the fifteenth and sixteenth century.

full legal advice and make sure you tick every box, CITES included (see the next page)!

Lastly, keep looking, keep learning and keep an eye open. Many of these items, as *Flog It!* bares testimony, are undervalued. You can put a very nice collection together for not a lot of money!

And, as a final word, it is important to mention CITES, the Convention on International Trade in Endangered Species of Wild Fauna and Flora, which is an international agreement between governments. It was set up to make sure that any trade in wild animals or plants doesn't, by effect, threaten their survival. An obvious example would be ivory. Your local auction house will be happy to give you proper advice.

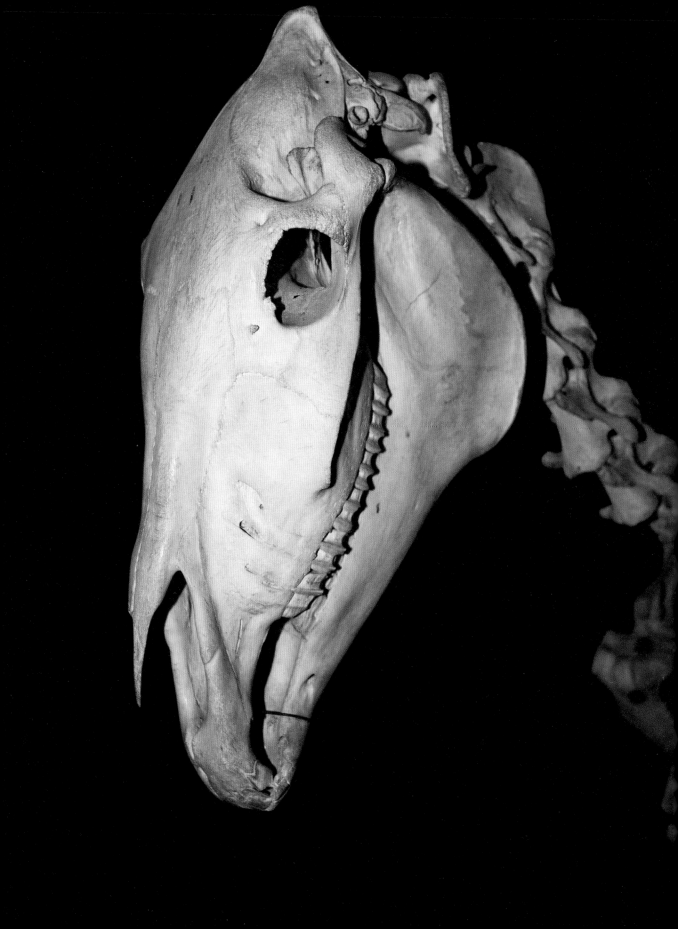

NATURAL HISTORY

Who didn't grow up fascinated by dinosaurs and fossils? I know I did and it's wonderful to see my kids exuding the exact same enthusiasm and fascination! And who hasn't jumped out of their seat whilst watching films like *The Lost World*, *100 Million Years BC* and, of course, the *Jurassic Park* films when a Tyrannosaurus Rex lumbered into view, stalking our hero while ripping into anything that moves.

Yet one of my favourite films is *Night at the Museum*. Who could forget the playful T Rex or the tetchy Triceratops skeletons? I think there's something really beautiful, almost sculptural, about the skeletal form and in September 2013 I visited Christie's Auction Rooms in South Kensington for a dinosaur experience with my son Dylan and my friend 'Uncle' Andrew. Dylan loves dinosaurs. No let me rephrase that, he lives dinosaurs! The auction was called 'Out of the Ordinary' and it sure was. It's not every day you see the complete skeleton of a cave bear from the upper Pleistocene period on display, a Woolly Mammoth tusk or, indeed,

what we really went to see, a triceratops skull.

The cave bear had been expected to make between £15,000 and £20,000 but in the end it reached £35,000 in the room! Then the Woolly Mammoth tusk made £37,500, again plus buyer's premium. Extraordinary! Then came the three-horned Triceratops skull and it made £193,875 plus buyer's premium, which is more than the average price of a terraced house in the UK, but there are plenty of terraced houses around – try finding another dinosaur skull! It was excavated in Hell Creek, Montana and the value of this sculptural time capsule will simply go up and up! Think about it for a minute, the age

of this skull is 65–70 million years! That's 65,000,000–70,000,000 if you want to show off the noughts. It lived at the end of the Cretaceous period, just before the mass extinction of the dinosaurs many scientists attribute to the asteroid that impacted Earth, causing the Chicxulub crater in the Yucatán Peninsula in Mexico. The resultant fall-out caused dust clouds to blot out the sunlight, resulting in climate change that ended the era of the dinosaurs.

Anyway, maybe you get the vibe? It sent a chill down my spine being so close to something so incredibly fascinating and, frankly, beautiful. It overwhelmed Dylan completely! Afterwards, 'Uncle' Andrew took us to the Natural History Museum, to see the baby woolly mammoth exhibition and the skeleton cast of Dippy the Diplodocus, who I'm sure many of you may remember seeing on a school trip back in the day. Wonderful as all the items on display are, nothing compared to the Triceratops head. The fact of the matter is that, if I'd left a bid, and the auctioneer called my maximum bid, in a crazy way it would have belonged to me for a few seconds! Of course, I didn't bid on the head. I'd love to own it, but really, wow, what a find.

So, now you understand my personal passion for skeletons! When I mention mammoths, please don't ever get them mixed up with elephants. We're talking about the excavated remains of an animal that died out at round 10,000 years ago. Yes, I know, there was a small colony of woolly mammoths that lived on until around 3,666 years ago on Wrangle Island, a Russian island in the Arctic Ocean about 600km west of Alaska, if my sums are correct! Elephants and rhinoceroses are covered by CITES and, in all likelihood, aside from the moral issues and my love of animals and utter contempt for anyone who could destroy such noble beasts, buying and selling ivory will probably, eventually, come under an international blanket ban, irrespective of its age.

I expect a few of you are thinking by now, 'Paul, why don't you get stuffed?' Well, let's talk about taxidermy then. I'll start by saying I don't like trophy wall mounts or anything shot or classified as big game. To me it's incredibly sad that animals should be killed for sport or to be used as ornaments and my personal opinion is, simply don't touch those sorts of things. However there is a growing market for indigenous (born and lived in the

UK) non-endangered species and taxidermy has enjoyed a resurgence in popularity in recent years. Interestingly, there are more women taxidermists than men and they are learning on squirrels and mice in the style of Walter Potter. Appropriately Walter made dioramas of animals that remind one of Beatrix Potter, although they were not related, with scenes of small creatures acting like humans – rabbit pupils in a school classroom and kittens getting married.

Has anyone been to Jamaica Inn on Bodmin Moor, where Daphne du Maurier set her novel of the same name? I used to go there with my parents to wonder at the many taxidermy items, which at one time included scenes created by Walter Potter. When the building was revamped, they sold off the inn curios in an auction. One curio I'm reminded of turned up in Mark Stacey's auction in Southend – a two-headed kitten which sold for around £700. Weird but enthralling!

I would say there are a lot of bad stuffed

birds and fish around, so don't bother with them. If your heart is set on an antique piece, look to Spicer for birds or Cooper for fish but truly, in my mind, it's better to invest in skeletons and anthropomorphic items.

I'm going to introduce you to a few skeletons that I personally own: a horse, a hippopotamus, a ram, a dog and a seal. My hippo's called Nicholas and he came up for sale at Adam Partridge's Sale Room, catalogued as the first hippo born in England, so no CITES certificate was needed. I booked a phone line having been tipped the

wink by Adam. He guessed my interest as I'd previously wanted to buy at Christie's in 2012 where Lot 55 was a hippo skull catalogued at £1,500–£2,500 in the Will Fisher sale, but it went above what I was prepared to pay and sold for £6,000.

So let me introduce Nicholas:

There I am two years later, on the phone to my friend Adam's auction rooms in Macclesfield while I was filming in Newcastle, one of my favourite cities. I've taken five minutes out to bid and I'm all fired up! This is my time, my skull, my sculptural

My good friend, Nicholas.

piece and while I've got my maximum bid in mind, I sensed this time the hippo wasn't going to get away. . . Nicholas, you're coming home! The feeling was immense, and the cost? I'd sold a couple of antiques to fund my dream and suddenly the bidding stops. Sold! To Paul Martin. What did I pay? £3,000. A couple of years later, he's almost like part of the family. Provenance was all, Nicholas had SUCH a history.

Zoos were so depressing in many ways and zoology wasn't really understood until relatively recently. However zoos did invoke a love of animals and ultimately our growing familiarity with the wonderful creatures exhibited resulted in worldwide outrage against poaching and, indeed, the conditions in which animals were kept. Their suffering may not have been in vain as I believe the lessons of the past have broadened our understanding of how things need to change and of the need to conserve our world. Longleat and Whipsnade's animals are happy and safe from poachers, but when you see any animals in cages it so depresses me. Nicholas, however, had a fully documented life thanks to his time in a zoo. He was certainly a personality and a much-loved hippo, having been born in Belle Vue Gardens Zoo on 5 December 1938. When he was just six years old in 1944, Nicholas made a sudden and unprovoked attack on his mother, burying his long tusks into her throat and neck and inflicting mortal injuries. He received a tusk to the head in the fight and the hole can be seen in his skull. The skull of his mother is now in the Manchester Museum with dimensions of: 70 x 47 x 55cm. However sad an end Nicholas met, the love he has had since and the appreciation my children have for his skull makes for a happy ending.

I was visiting a dealer when I saw the most remarkable skeleton of a horse mounted on a large black plinth, clearly prepared for display by a taxidermist who knew about anatomy. Will Fisher, founder of his company Jamb, has his showroom in Pimlico in London where he exhibits amongst other things, sculptural pieces. The horse had been created as an educational display for vets, much like the human skeletons used in human anatomy. I had been driving by one night and it almost fluoresced at me in the glare of passing headlights as if to say, 'Come on, what are you waiting for?'

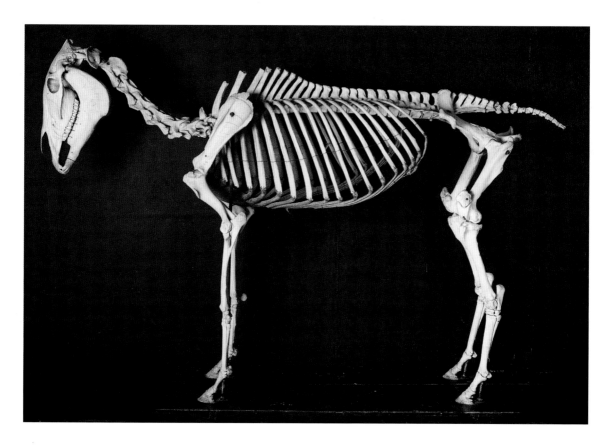

like some latter day Mr Ed, Hollywood's talking horse. Maybe you've had moments like that – you either have to pull up as soon as you can, or you turn around and dash back. I rationalised to my wife that Nicholas needed a friend! I'll be honest, it took some explaining and I'm not going to underplay how shocked she was, seeing a skeleton of a horse appear! Her expression seemed to say 'What next?' in the sort of way only a loved one can express. After the horse, along came a regimental ram followed swiftly by a French seal. Maybe it's an addiction, maybe I'm addicted to buying antiques? Well I suppose it is a gamble, but then sometimes the pay-back is huge and you're never likely to lose everything you've invested!

By the way, the seal came from an auction room in Godalming called Summers Place. What am I like? Well, a few weeks later, I thought 'Oh, wow! A boxer dog!' Someone in the Edwardian era couldn't be parted from their beloved dog, so they had it preserved for display – a lovely piece of taxidermy. I think

The Scrimshaw from aboard the HMS Beagle.

you probably know how much of a dog lover I am. When my lovely old German Shepherd, Bluebell, died I was truly distraught and so I empathised with the owner of the boxer. It's like losing a member of the family, they're such loyal and wonderful company. Listen, if you feel this is all a little bit macabre, how many of you have visited natural history exhibitions? Well, to me, it's the same. There's a connection and an emotion, yet the natural world has also produced such beautiful structures in the skeletons of every animal.

As a footnote, taxidermy is enjoying a renaissance, with, as I mentioned, more women (predominantly aged eighteen to thirty-five) filling the classes than any other group.

If you watch *Flog It!* regularly, you will be quite familiar with Scrimshaws. Scrimshaws were predominantly made from ivory or shell. I know I have said 'Don't touch ivory' in big, bold, huge, enormous letters, because elephant ivory disgusts me, but these items come from a different age – the age of seafarers – and have nothing to do with elephants at all. Scrimshaws were generally carved by seamen or natives of the Arctic region, picking out intricate shapes of animals or fancy designs in the surface of the tusks, bones or teeth of whales, walruses or other large sea creatures. They are sometimes considered folk art, while other people label them ethnographica but surely they all have a place in Natural History?

Recently, a rare and important scrim-shawed sperm whale's tooth by James Adolphus Bute, a Royal Marine on HMS *Beagle*, went under the hammer. The *Beagle*, of course, was the ship that took naturalist Charles Darwin on his voyage of discovery in 1831. Let's look at how it was catalogued by auctioneer Adam Partridge and see if we can assess whether it was worth a bid?

'The face is engraved with a family of Fuegians in a canoe, possibly the four native Fuegians who were taken back to England in 1830 known as Jemmy Button, Fuegia Basket, York Minster &

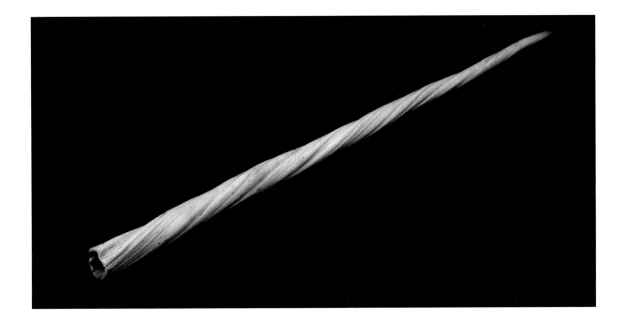

Boat Memory, above title 'Canoe Indians Beagle Channel Tierra del Fuego'; the reverse engraved with an island landscape titled 'Queen's Island Tahiti', with white metal mounts for use as a snuff mull, length 20cm (8 inches). James Adolphus Bute was born in England around 1799 and joined the Royal Navy as a Marine Private c.1819; he is listed as a marine on board the Beagle's famous voyage on which Charles Darwin spent five years of his survey trip to South America. Darwin's most influential work *On the Origin of the Species* was based on the findings of this trip. The tooth is most likely to have been obtained from the whaling station on The Falkland Islands and there are only five other known examples of Bute's scrimshaw. The most recent was sold at Bonhams Auctioneers in London on 16th September 2009 for £34,000. PROVENANCE: Thomas Burgess, Royal Marine aboard HMS Beagle on this voyage and thence by direct descent to the present owner. This lot is accompanied by three copies of letters written by Thos Burgess to his parents Israel Burgess of Heaton Norris near Stockport.'

It certainly was worth a bid! Hammer price: £6,000.

This Narwhal tusk (pictured above) would have enthralled a nineteenth-century audience as they were often displayed or sold as unicorn tusks. This lot is accompanied by a note of provenance stating that this tusk was purchased by the Wellcome Foundation c.1910

Here you can see the fossils of trilobites in the rock.

for use at agricultural shows for advertising purposes. The Wellcome Foundation was established by Henry Wellcome and became the largest pharmaceutical company in the world. The unicorn was the logo of the Wellcome Foundation from 1908-95. The tusks were used by the company until 1980 when the company ceased making veterinary drugs and stopped attending shows. All the advertising material was put into storage at the company headquarters in Crewe Hall, a fabulous Jacobean mansion in Cheshire that is now a luxury hotel. When the company moved from Crewe, all of this material was disposed of by the contractors and this tusk was salvaged by the vendor.

Hammer price: £14,500.

While considering my collection of skeletons, what about fossils and what about our Jurassic coastline? I can't believe I haven't already mentioned it! It is perfect! With coastal erosion comes an ever-advancing window into the past and the area has inspired some of our greatest scientists and researchers.

I'm all for a collection that you can start

for nothing. Go and look at some ordinary gravel, you'll most likely find tiny fossilised trilobites (like woodlice), shells and tiny fronds of bracken. Remember, too, that our chalk downlands were once a tropical sea bed. Fossils and finds are everywhere! But please stay away from the cliff edge as falls are common, not so much you falling over the edge, but rocks that can suddenly and unexpectedly break away, falling on you as you forage below. And under no circumstances should you hammer at the cliff – that can easily bring a section crashing down on your head. So keep your fossil hunting to the sea shore and if you are taking a little hammer to break open objects, always wear goggles! Better still, why not join one of the fossil hunting groups that can give information and advice to help you enjoy our past and your new interest. You never know, someone reading this might be inspired to start fossil hunting and suddenly find themselves celebrated as the new Mary Anning. Who's Mary? Well I'll introduce to her if you haven't already heard of her…

Mary lived in a time of change, with the Industrial Revolution under way and much of the globe painted pink to indicate the British Empire, yet her interest lay in the past and indeed, the beauty of the Dorset coast. Along with her brother Joseph, Mary spent her childhood hunting for fossils. Little did she know that aged just twelve the world would come to focus its attention on her for the

The infamous ichthyosaur.

extraordinary finds she and her sibling made. Together their most memorable find has to be the ichthyosaur skull. It was 1.2m long and, as this was 1811, let's use imperial measure, that's 4 feet. They subsequently unearthed the rest of the 17-foot (5.2m) skeleton – that's as long as a Ford Transit van, or a posh horse-drawn carriage in Mary's day. It took Mary and Joseph a year to excavate and I'm going to say with every pun intended, that truly is a biblical effort!

Mary's passion changed our perceptions of the past and she became renowned worldwide as a fossil hunter extraordinaire, a dealer and, indeed, a palaeontologist who worked along the coast at Lyme Regis. She went on to discover two plesiosaur skeletons, even bigger than her ichthyosaur, a pterosaur (the first skeleton of this creature found outside of Germany) and numerous fish fossils. While fossil hunting was fashionable, during her life Mary struggled financially and for academic recognition of her work, not least because the misogynistic attitudes of the day prevented her from joining any societies, such as the Geological Society of London, simply because she was a woman.

Now, for all the Mary and Josephs out there, I might sound like an exponent of the nanny state, but please, please, please be very careful when you are hunting for fossils. It almost cost Mary her life when a rock fall killed her dog. So please take note and please be warned! However, if you stay safe and indulge your passion, think on this too; a tyrannosaurus rex tooth sold at Bonhams for a shade under £9,000, not including buyer's premium.

Mary sadly passed away in 1847 at the age of just forty-seven as a result of breast cancer, but her legacy and knowledge has left its mark. Today, most towns have a shop selling crystals and gems, with a huge ammonite in the window, sometimes a tray of fossilised sharks' teeth and perhaps some amber and jet. Our passion is in part thanks to Mary who educated our ancestors to understand that there were millions of years pre-humanity when strange beasts roamed the earth.

Not only can you find fossils when fossicking on the shoreline, but also some naturally occurring treasures that may or may not be worth a great deal but certainly make excellent, collectible souvenirs. We're blessed in Britain to have one of the most well-known locations to find jet, Whitby. The word seems synonymous with the much-sought-after black jewellery, the mainstay of Victorian mourning. William Hammond opened the first Whitby jet shop in Whitby in 1860 and it's still there today. Jet jewellery values vary but an antique piece will probably be worth somewhere around £1,200 retail for a fine necklace. Jet is a mineraloid which means it has an organic origin so it's not considered by gemologists to be a true mineral. It is in fact a type of lignite or fossilised wood – essentially the same stuff as coal – that comes from something similar to a monkey puzzle tree. Jet is found all over the world, but the finest quality is recognised as coming from Whitby along the north east coast of Yorkshire. There are seams of jet that appear at sea level, often

The rather odd, but highly valuable ambergris.

extending right under the sea bed. Natural erosion and heavy storms sometimes cause chunks of jet to break away and that is where you will find it being washed up on the beach.

Amber is a fossilised tree resin that often contains leaf fronds or tiny insects, made famous in *Jurassic Park* films as the basis from which cells were removed to clone living creatures. Although it occurs all over the world, the finest is perhaps found in Southwold, on the Suffolk coast. Orangey brown in colour it's sometimes faked using plastic resin, so do be careful and check the item over thoroughly.

One bizarre substance that commands huge values at auction is, wait for it, whale vomit. Again, washed up on beaches, known rather more academically as ambergris, it is

An example of jet, turned jewellery.

found in the stomachs of sperm whales and it is believed that it coats irritating matter in the whale's stomach. Eventually it is either vomited or passes through the whale's system to be ejected as whale excrement. Nice! Now before anyone screws their nose up and thinks I'm being low-brow for the sake of amusing editorial, you might like to know that it has been used in the manufacture of perfume for centuries as it helps to trap fragrances on the skin. I must add again that it is illegal to trade in the substance as it could have been obtained from killing a whale, but when it is washed up on a beach it is quite legal to sell it on, perhaps at auction.

Auctioneer Adam Partridge sold a piece that had been found by someone beachcombing in Anglesey. It was conservatively estimated at £5,000–£7,000, weighing in at just over a kilo. I'll copy in what the catalogue said:

RARE WHALE VOMIT TO BE AUCTIONED

An extremely rare sample of whale vomit, also known as ambergris, is to be sold at Adam Partridge Auctioneers in Macclesfield, Cheshire. The 1.1kg specimen was discovered by a dog walker on a beach in Anglesey, North Wales.

Ambergris is formed in the stomach of a sperm whale and is thought to be produced to protect the whale's insides from sharp squid beaks (squid being the sperm whale's main source of food). The substance is then secreted either as vomit, or with faeces. Over time, it hardens and has been known to wash up on beaches, usually in the Caribbean, often still containing squid beaks.

Because of its unpleasant beginnings, it could perhaps be considered surprising that the main use humans have for it is in perfume. For centuries, it has been used as a 'fixative' which makes the perfume last longer on skin. A whole chapter is devoted to it in Herman Melville's *Moby-Dick*, where it is exclaimed 'Who would think, then, that such fine ladies and gentlemen should regale themselves with an essence found in the inglorious bowels of a sick whale!'

Adam had never seen ambergris before in all of his years in the business: 'We've had lots of unusual items pass through the doors over the years, but this is by far the weirdest,' he said. 'Ambergris can be worth as much as gold, but just like gold it very much depends on the purity. The estimates of £5,000 to £7,000 are fairly conservative and if this is of the highest quality, then it could fetch five figures.'

So there you have it! Next time you pass a drunk who's been sick on platform two I want you to think to yourself, 'Why aren't they whales?'

The greatest collector of natural history who has ever lived, certainly the grandfather of cataloguing and identifying, is Charles Darwin and you really should visit the collection housed at the Natural History Museum if you get the opportunity. Having embarked on HMS *Beagle* in 1831, he spent five years sailing around the globe, picking up specimens to study, identify, catalogue and compare. Darwin concluded that we are all the product of natural selection; in other words we can trace back the origin of species through the breeding process. This opinion caused outrage and in some quarters it still does, with Darwin seen as heretic. However, his collection and his writing, which can be viewed online incidentally, is worth a read, if only as a natural historical document of huge merit.

Almost 6ft tall and awkward in his movements, Darwin stood out from the crowd. His love of nature had flourished as a child, when he spent hours walking in North Wales. He attended medical school in Edinburgh but the sight of blood repelled him and he left before completing his studies! His father insisted he attend Christ's College, Cambridge to study theology but Darwin spent more time collecting bugs, choosing them over his then love interest, Fanny, who broke off their relationship due to the amount of time Charles spent indulging his passion for wildlife.

Darwin's influences were many, yet it was probably John Henslow whom we can thank for the direction Charles's life took as it was he who recommended Darwin for a place on HMS *Beagle*. Darwin's famous book

known as *The Origin of Species* but actually lumbered with the far less snappy title of *On the Origin of Species by Means of Natural Selection, or the Preservation of Favoured Races in the Struggle for Life* was published in 1859 to immediate vitriol and intense argument between scientists and theologians; they're still arguing today! Scientists argued for the logic of natural selection and evolution, while those with religious convictions maintained that God created everything. After a long illness, Charles passed away in 1882 and was buried at Westminster Abbey. On the day of his funeral, it was said that the Archbishop was indisposed.

The whole hoo-ha, the scientific analysis and just about everything else about Darwin's work provoked a huge interest in collecting specimens from the natural world. Everyone wanted their own little museum of curios which, considering the fact that they were natural, in other words to be found in nature, made collecting accessible to a wider public. Yes, there were bound to be things in which only the rich could indulge, but anyone with a keen eye could start collecting and the same is true today.

So what should you buy and avoid? Don't touch ivory, avoid it like the plague and avoid badly stuffed animals too. There is too much bad taxidermy out there and it has forced prices down. Also, you need to display birds under glass, while a skeleton will display wonderfully as a sculptural piece simply on a plinth or, if it's a skull, just sitting on a table or sideboard. Oh, and in general, avoid collecting eggs, too.

Tips? Skeletons with provenance, in other words written proof of where it came from and what the animal was called, anything that gives a history, are preferable. Jet and amber? Ensure they are the real thing and, in the case of amber, gravitate towards pieces with insects or flora trapped inside. I suppose one final note on taxidermy would be to amend my thoughts on 'bad taxidermy' simply to say that once in a while a piece comes up that was really badly done, in fact so badly done that it makes everyone smile and by effect, makes it collectible in its own right.

Okay, so you're all wondering what the whale vomit made. . . have a guess! £11,000, or the price of a reasonable second hand car, a family holiday or a rather nice bathroom!

Keep looking, keep thinking and enjoy the things you collect.

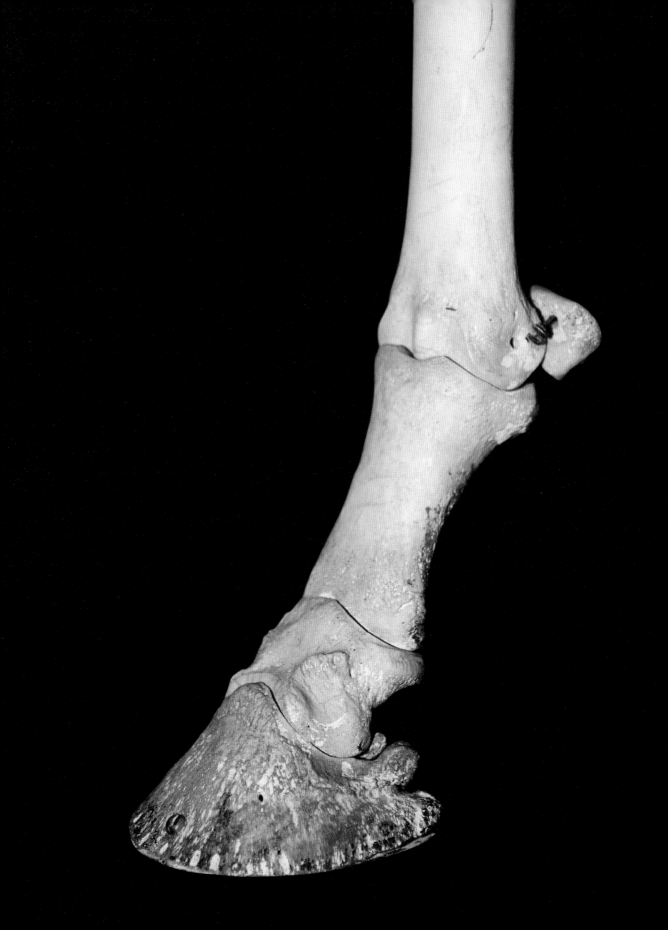

MIRROR, MIRROR ON THE WALL

Mention Arthur Negus and *Going for a Song* and my friend's auntie would always call out 'Going for a snog!', such was the affection everyone had for this charming man. Had it not been for Arthur's personality and the show's long-running success there probably wouldn't ever have been shows like *Flog It! Going for a Song* was an antiques quiz show first broadcast in 1965 and it made a star out of sixty-two-year-old Arthur, who had spent a lifetime learning about antiques and became a household name at an age when most people are looking forward to retirement!

He was the resident antique and furniture expert on the show and although the series was initially presented by Max Robertson, Arthur was the reason the show became the success it did. He was also an author, dealer and such a character too, learning his trade through his time with auctioneers Bruton, Knowles and Co. of Gloucester. Although born in Reading he developed what I can only describe as a West Country accent which the public loved! He was awarded the OBE, had the honour of being the butt of Monty Python jokes and even appeared on *The Generation Game* to rapturous applause.

Arthur was a true gentleman and his interest in furniture triggered my own fascination as I sat at home with mum and dad, all of us entranced by his knowledge, little realising that one day, I would be on television talking about antiques, just like Arthur! He inspired my love of antiques as I developed a fascination for period furniture and, in particular, mirrors, of which I have a small collection. I wanted to write a whole chapter about mirrors and started jotting down a few notes here and there; this made me realise how little is written about things just about everyone on the planet uses every day!

From time immemorial people have glanced at their reflections in everything from pools of water, pieces of polished obsidian, ice and even conkers, tree sap and tomatoes, with mirrors considered a luxury item up until really quite recently. Glass mirrors coated with a metal process were being made by artisans in Sidon, Lebanon almost 2,500

An incredible example of an Etruscan bronze mirror, from the 3rd-2nd century BC.

years ago, but they would have been simple face mirrors and far too expensive a possession for the average person. Polished bronze mirrors were made in Egypt even earlier with examples dating back some 4,500 years, while in Britain, the 2,000-year-old Desborough mirror offers us a glimpse into the past, its exquisite design and engraved back showing the exemplary craftsmanship that our Celtic ancestors possessed. The designs of the Celts were quite different to those of the Roman invaders whose mirrors were less intricately carved yet had a more recognisable style, often copied in the eighteenth century for their classical simplicity.

It would appear that, while the Celts were amazing craftsmen they also seem to have been incredibly vain, very much liking the look of themselves. According to Cassius Dio, who published a history of Rome in eighty volumes, the wife of Argentocoxus, who came from the Scottish borders, made a rather cheeky aside to Julia Augusta, wife of the Emperor. She joked to the Empress, 'We fulfill the demands of nature in a much better way than do you Roman women; for we consort openly with the best men, whereas you let yourselves be debauched in secret by the vilest.' Clearly she believed that looks mattered more than personality and so one can only think that personal grooming and dress sense played as important a role then as it does today. But what a superficial, narcissistic lot. If they'd had Internet dating back then, we might still be governed by the Druids!

Celtic designs would once more find favour when interpreted by the Arts and Crafts movement in the late nineteenth century and then again from the late twentieth

And one from the British
Isles, the infamous
Desborough Mirror.

century onwards, when every New Age shop in Glastonbury and Avebury sells reproductions of Celtic designs to visitors entranced by paganism and Celtic back-to-nature philosophy.

'Scrying bowls' were a kind of mirror used to foretell the future. A fluid was poured into the receptacle and the reflection used to divine whatever mystical message was sought. Water was commonly used, but I've also heard of liquid mercury being used too, with the bowl itself sometimes carved out of agate or amethyst to heighten the reflectivity of the liquid. Scrying comes from the Old English word 'descry', which meant 'to dimly reveal'. From ancient Egypt, Greece and China to the druids, eighteenth-century aristocrats and nineteenth-century mystics like the Russian occultist Madame Blavatsky, the desire to glimpse the future and sometimes the past reflected society's obsession with lifting the veil of the unknown. The mystical properties of mirrors made them objects of fascination and Pope John XII stated that 'The Devil can conceal himself in … a mirror' and priests were forbidden to own one! Although Pope John XII died in 964AD the Middle Ages became a dark time for mirrors.

The 'curse' of mirrors came from the way they were used for occult 'scrying' purposes and I'm drawn to remember an old 1974 Peter Cushing film *From Beyond the Grave*, where he plays an antiques dealer who sells a mirror that traps the soul of the buyer. The film is split into four stories and in the segment called 'The Gatecrasher,' the buyer cheats the seller (Cushing) out of the mirror for a much reduced price by convincing him it's a reproduction, which of course it isn't! Once at home in proud possession of the mirror, the new owner, played wonderfully by actor David Warner (who I'm sure you know from *The Omen*, *Titanic*, *Cross of Iron* and *Star Trek* and a host of other movies), decides to hold a séance. He is forced to carry out some very grizzly deeds by a demon in the mirror, before his spirit is trapped inside it, thus releasing an evil entity into the world in human form. The basis of this story is in the folk lore of the reflection, but you have been warned! Before we move on, think about the mysticism of the mirror in our popular culture with films like *Snow White and the Seven Dwarfs*, *The Mirror Crack'd*, *Mirror, Mirror* and *Oculus*. And let's be honest, when it comes to mirrors, men are just as proportionally vain as women! Who remembers nightclubs in the 1980s when every disco from Aberdeen to Southampton was mirrored from wall to wall, Liberty's started selling distressed mirrored tables and every boutique had one wall completely mirrored, too?

Anyway, way back in time again, by the eleventh century clear glass mirrors were being made in Spain by the Moors, although these were still hand-sized and nothing like the huge mirrors we have become used to today. By the fifteenth century, Murano mirror glass was being incorporated into

An example of a Spanish mirror from the mid-1700s.

religious icons and reliquaries to catch the light and illuminate the icon or picture as though a shaft of light had appeared from Heaven. Murano was one of the Venetian islands and the birthplace of commercial mirror-making in Europe, the Venetians having protected the secrets of their glass-making processes by offering glass-makers great rewards for keeping their techniques under wraps – with anyone who blabbed, or even attempted to leave Venice, facing a death sentence! By the Elizabethan age craftsmen from Murano had made it out alive and were working across Europe, including in London, sharing the secret of making rolled plate glass which was, of course, then framed into the designs we call mirrors. After The Restoration in 1660, when gaudy extravagance was back in vogue following the coronation of Charles II after years of puritanical austerity, mirrors edged in tapestry often depicting biblical or animal scenes became the 'must have' trend of the rich.

With the use of new materials came more and more ornate frames, made of carved wood or indeed gesso, where cast plaster is applied to the wooden surface and then gilded, burnished or occasionally painted. Once the technology with which the glass blower could create a rolled glass plate had been developed, the glass needed grinding. This process involved fixing the plate to a horizontal bench. To simplify what the process entails, I'll try and explain it thus; basically the glass is sprinkled with fine sand and water. Another plate is then eased into position. The top plate has a box on top that is filled with heavy stones, so considering the pressure, you can imagine this to be a very skilled job in order to avoid the plates cracking or breaking. The two plates are worked together and as the polishing process smooths the plates down, the sand is washed out and replaced with even finer sand, and then eventually something called smalt which, if I'm right, is a cobalt blue potassium glass that grinds the glass even further. That's not it, either! Once the grinding has taken place, we're on to the polishing. The polishing is done with a block and putty and emery and something called 'triple'. By the mid-1800s steam engines accelerated the rubbing and polishing process.

The silvering process is next. This was undertaken using a hare's foot (I'm not making this up) to create an incredibly thin layer of mercury on the back of the glass that makes it reflective rather than transparent. So let's visualise this and look at it again: first the glass blower cut the top of the bubble he had blown, then skilfully laid the glass on a flat bed rolling out a plate with a flat rod. It was then hand-ground to make it smooth. Imagine the dust going in your eyes and face. Any bevel on the glass was never really sharp. Then they applied the mercury coating.

Once the cabinet makers and gesso makers had done their job, they passed the mirror and the frame to the gilders, but in time all of these craftsmen would be affected by the mercury which damaged their lungs, kidneys and brains, impairing their speech, vision, hearing and coordination. It's not for me either to justify or criticise the industrial injuries of 300 years ago, but when we consider the average age of death was around forty, I like to believe mirror makers enjoyed their work and that, as valued trades, the negatives were far outweighed by the positives, such as the lifestyle afforded to their families. Dying for one's art may sound macabre, but consider too the reality that drinking water was often filthy, food putrid and stale and if you look in any pre-twentieth-century cemetery you'll see the graves of countless children who lived in such a poisoned age that many didn't make it beyond a few months old. Manpower, I suppose, was relatively cheap and materials quite expensive as opposed to today, of course, when labour costs are expensive and the materials relatively cheap. A quality mirror of 52 inches in Chippendale's time cost 53 pounds, 5 shillings and 6 pence – more than twice the annual income of many families – and you can see how a fancy mirror was only ever likely to be something the wealthy elite could afford.

I must stress that, once sealed in the frame, mercury mirrors pose no airborne contaminant and unless you smash it apart and start licking the back of the glass it's as safe as a mirror made yesterday. I know which I prefer! So is it repro or is it period? One way of discerning this is to rub your thumb down the bevel, if it has one. If it's smooth and faultless, it's probably reproduction.

Of course today, most people don't fancy a hard grind followed by a slow polish just to look at themselves in the mirror. So what are the options? Who hasn't been to a DIY outlet only to be disappointed and come home with something flimsy that cracks when you try screwing it to the wall, or fractures when your auntie leans on it while brushing her hair one August Bank Holiday? Then there are fashion mirrors made out of expanded resin and foams that seem to flake after a year or two and never look quite as glamorous as they did in the shop. So what's my suggestion? Need you ask? Of course! Go and buy an antique mirror that will add character to your home and which may eventually go up in value. The reality of the current market is that you can buy a beautiful eighteenth or nineteenth century mirror for a few hundred pounds at auction, while seventeenth century mirrors are at last affordable.

Charles I mirrors were only available in small-sized tapestry or tortoise shell frames with royal and biblical scenes popular. Gold and silver thread was worked intricately, then surrounded by a walnut frame. Since the time of Charles II, the body of the mirror has almost always been pine, primarily because its open, coarse grain allowed veneers to stick to it so well. During the reign of William and Mary, mirrors were still the domain of the elite, but marquetry frames became popular with intricate designs and inlays.

William Kent was a renowned furniture maker of the early eighteenth century whose work was destined for Chiswick House, Hampton Court Palace and Stowe, his designs exuding the Palladian style which he's attributed with developing in Britain, although in fairness he took the idea from sixteenth-century Venetian architect Andrea Palladio. But let's be honest, he was hugely inspired by the classical Roman architecture so prevalent in Italy, and as some people say, 'there's nothing's new' as an idea or concept. Yet no one can detract from either Palladio or Kent whose designs and concepts were extraordinary.

William Kent designed and made large mirrors, predominantly rectangular in gilt wood, which simply means carved wood that has been gilded. He introduced acanthus leaves and applique flowers and wonderful egg and dart mouldings, outset corners and architectural pediments to follow the form of the neoclassical buildings being commissioned by the aristocracy. Kent's designs were inspired by Rome and the mirror would often emulate the kinds of niches that might have housed the statue of a Roman emperor, yet through his designs, YOU were the emperor – your reflection was the grand statue to be admired. Expect to pay £10,000 for a fine pair 'in the

manner of Kent' mirrors and if you can find an original documented piece, the prices are considerable. There are plenty of nineteenth-century William Kent-inspired pieces around and, of course, because the designs were recycled, if you are going for 'the look' it's not going to cost the earth if you go for late Victorian copies. For investment pieces, you guessed it, always buy the best you can.

Chippendale mirrors come in a variety of styles as we know, but the wonderful Chinese Chippendale style makes a fantastic mirror.

An embroidered mirror frame edged with tortoiseshell, c.1665

An exquisite Charles II carved and painted mirror.

Pier mirrors were made to sit between doorways in pairs and generally came in trios with the mirror, a torcher and a tall cabinet or stand. If you've visited a stately home or watched *Downton Abbey* or indeed thumbed through *Country Life*, you'll be familiar with the way the mirrors were used to bounce light and help illuminate a room once the candles were lit (no tallow here). Whilst chandeliers were only designed to light themselves, torchers and mirrors were used to illuminate rooms. Chippendale mirrors, like his furniture, come in a multitude of designs and were copied, like Kent's designs,

in the late nineteenth century and even in the present day in resin and expanding foam. You know which I'll go for!

All good joiners and cabinet makers had mirrors listed on their calling card and occasionally you'll find one such card tucked in the back of a mirror. Believe me when I say that occasionally these can be worth more than the mirror, while also adding provenance and desirability.

So here we are, around about three hundred years later and the original mirror glass is showing signs of its age. The mercury has discoloured and the mirror may even be crazed and non-reflective. So what should you do? I know what hundreds of people do every year. They have the glass replaced with modern glass and the restorer, if he is worth his salt, will put the original glass to one side, probably marrying it up to another period frame! Why? Because the aging of the glass is exactly what you should look for. Imagine the candle and gas light these mirrors have lived through. Imagine the dramas and love affairs, the historical moments and the social history they have reflected. Imagine, too, that you've something untouched and original hanging on your wall. Well, here's my simple advice. Leave it as it is. Don't have it restored and under no circumstances should you replace the glass with modern glass – it will devalue it and turn something magical into just another eighteenth-century frame.

Mirrors are my tip as an investment. There are lots of French and continental mirrors on sale in shops and auction rooms and don't get me wrong, they can be hugely valuable and wonderfully beautiful, but look out for English eighteenth-century mirrors with, of course, the original glass. Charles II mirrors with their tapestry frames and Queen Anne

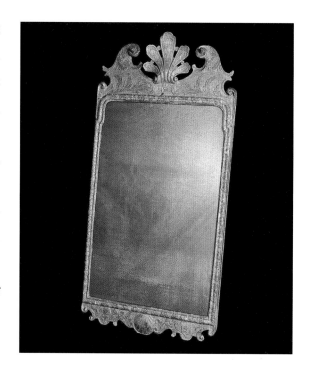

Interior design in the style of Thomas Kent.

mirrors with their William Kent style are my favourite. Travelling mirrors were popular in the eighteenth century and were often leather framed. Liberty copper mirrors of the Arts and Crafts with their Ruskin ceramic appliques are worth a look, too. Get it, worth a look? Whatever your perception of antiques, never ever succumb to the idea that they are simply there for academics to intellectualise over. That was rarely the intention of the craftsman. They were there to be used and it saddens me when people present the most wonderful items on *Flog It!* but lack the confidence to display them in their homes. Most people are selling things because they have inherited or been given an item they don't particularly like. However, there are always people whose eyes light up when told a story and it heartens me when they decide to keep something of important social history to their family.

I guess my only proviso would be, if you have young children, keep your investments, especially mirrors and ceramics, away from play areas! That probably goes without saying really, but a couple of personal experiences saw my inquisitive children break a few things, quite unintentionally. Of course if this

happens you only have yourself to blame! By the same token, antique furniture is often quite resilient and has already lived through generation after generation of children and probably survived very well. Indeed, in the case of folk art, the wear and age related marks are a bonus. I'm trying to say that antiques should be used and loved, not left in some sterile environment, but be sensible and think rationally about how and where you display and use things. Also, when buying a mirror, don't get put off by a split

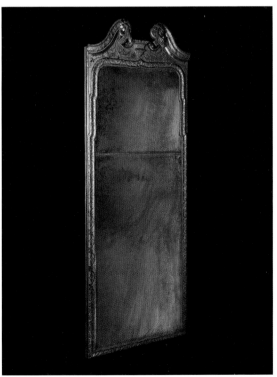

Imagine the stories behind these slightly damaged panes, and the care taken in trying to repair them...

Chippendale at its finest.

The glass might have dulled with age, but that doesn't detract from its splendour.

More recently, and I can't believe I haven't mentioned him so far, fictional antique dealer Lovejoy in the TV series based on the books by Jonathan Gash, has a whole episode in series five titled 'Who Is the Fairest of Them All?' which is devoted pretty much entirely to mirrors! In the plot, a young girl having ballet lessons becomes terrified by a mirror at the Ballet School, so Lovejoy, Eric and Tinker spend most of the episode looking for a suitable mirror with which to replace it. Meanwhile, the deliciously aristocratic Lady Jane, played sublimely by Phyllis Logan, breaks Lovejoy's heart, leaving the series for pastures new. I mention this episode in passing as in the story, Lovejoy visits an antique shop that specialises in mirrors and the owner, played wonderfully by the late, great English actor Roger Lloyd-Pack, has some 'ladies who lunch and antique' in the shop, interested in buying a mirror with exquisitely aged glass. Of course, Lovejoy saves the sale as they have pooh-poohed the oxidised and aged mirror plate as unusable, and he arranges to have the mirror plate replaced, popping the old glass into another mirror, naturally, which, if my memory serves me right, Tinker commandeers from an aunt!

plate. In other words the glass looks like two mirrors put together. This might be an estate repair, where a mirror was broken during some uproarious house party, or a cleaning accident, and the maintenance man had some old glass from another 'incident' that he cut and placed together to create a plate of the correct size. It might even be the craftsman using this expensive resource, making two pier mirrors which he would match along the split. Remember the value mirror glass had 300 years ago?

An exerpt from the *Director*.

Back in the real world, Ronald Phillips is one of England's top antique dealers and his showroom is in Bruton Street, London. It's an Aladdin's cave of statement pieces, particularly mirrors, predominantly eighteenth-century, although Ronald has some extraordinary mirrors from the seventeenth and early nineteenth centuries, too. Have a look at his website as, aside from it being his market place for the shop, it's a wonderful educational tool and the stock photos will give you a masterclass in what to look for in a period mirror.

One of my favourite mirror-makers of the early part of the eighteenth century is John Vardy, whose gilt gesso mirrors had some of the William Kent style, with architectural pediments and cartouches. His mirrors were often quite geometric and in my mind almost pre-empted the Regency and Empire styles by more than half a century.

Of course, Thomas Chippendale is, was and always will be one of the greatest mirror designers ever, as was fellow eighteenth-century cabinet maker and designer John Linnell, whose business was based at 28 Berkeley Square in London's West End. His trade mark was the use of cartouches and garlands that hung in swags across the mirror plate. Although by their era some mirror plates were being produced in Vauxhall, London, both Thomas and John imported mirror plates from France.

By 1835 the Germans had developed a process where silver was used to back mirrors, which revolutionised the mirror-making process and banished the use of mercury from all but the most diehard workshops.

Then, as the glass-making industry became more mechanised, it became possible to mass produce mirrors and accordingly, the price went down. As technology developed, so the bevel became silky smooth and eventually took on the almost flawless quality even the cheapest mirrors appear to have today.

For me the whole process, the design and the inherent flaws of old glass mirrors are what makes them attractive. They are, after all, the most wonderfully tactile and emotive of furnishing items, bringing any room to life as they catch even the briefest of movements. Next time you look in a mirror, I hope you'll think of all the people who've brushed their hair, checked their makeup and adjusted their clothes whilst looking at their reflection and if you're fortunate enough to find yourself looking into an eighteenth-century mirror or earlier, think of all the social history it's seen and contemplate the fact that it was carved and made by a craftsman who had no concepts of MDF or laser cutting. It was painstakingly made by hand using all the processes we've looked at and it was copied from designs that were laboriously drawn using the inspirations of ancient Greece and Rome.

Meet the Experts: Will Axon

Will Axon first appeared on our screens as a fresh-faced new kid on the block in 2005, having been talent-spotted auctioneering at a televised sale. Since then, he has appeared alongside Paul as a regular on-screen expert for *Flog It!*, taken a ride or two in a classic car for *Antiques* and *Celebrity Antiques Road Trip*, and gone head-to-head against other familiar faces for *Put Your Money Where Your Mouth Is*. He is yet to be beaten!

Born in Newmarket, Suffolk, Will worked for some of the country's leading provincial salerooms before returning to where it all started, to head up Rowley's Antiques and Fine Art Auctioneers. A small independent firm, Rowley's punches above its weight with outstanding sale results and a growing international reputation, holding quarterly fine-art and antiques sales at the world-famous Tattersalls Sale Ring in Newmarket and providing both private and corporate clients with a confidential professional service across East Anglia and beyond.

Will's most memorable discoveries off-screen include a pair of eighteenth-century carved marble figures of Vulcan and Venus by Sir Henry Cheere, which he stumbled across during a valuation on behalf of a local charity. After a mix of both private and trade bidding across eleven telephone lines and in the room, they sold for £450,000, which, at the time, was one of the highest prices achieved by any saleroom outside London.

Will's most important rediscovery came about when, while clearing a house in Cambridge, he uncovered a nineteenth-century Gothic Revival-painted pine sideboard designed by the illustrious English architect and designer William Burges. The whereabouts of this remarkable piece – painted with Bacchic scenes by the artist Nathaniel Westlake – were unrecorded since it was exhibited in the Medieval Court at the 1862 International Exhibition. It now resides in the Art Institute of Chicago, having sold for £250,000, a record price for English-painted pine furniture at the time.

On screen, Will's favourite find has to be the pair of size 42 giant leather boots brought in to *Flog It!* when filming at Wells Cathedral. Never having seen another pair, Will advised the sellers to pitch them at a low estimate and let the market decide what they were worth, though he had a sneaky suspicion that the boots could touch four figures. On the day, bidding started in the tens, proceeded through the hundreds and hit the thousands, finally selling for £3,600!

If money were no object, Will would collect early English oak and vernacular country furniture, early English pottery and Old Master drawings, mixed in with a few modern pieces too, of course. He just needs the country stately home to house it all and a rich sponsor!

Meet the Experts: Michael Baggott

Michael started collecting antiques when he was ten years old and the passion soon turned into a career when, after school, he left for college to study fine-art valuation, gaining experience working in the silver departments of Phillips Knowle and Christie's in London before heading up the silver department at Sotheby's in Billingshurst for four happy years. He then branched out to become a specialist dealer in silver and works of art alongside consulting for many of the large UK salerooms. He has written and researched many articles on antique silver and is the author of *An Illustrated Guide to York Hallmarks 1776–1858 & A Transcript and Index of the York Assay Office Ledger 1805–1821*.

'Ever since I can remember, antiques have been an endless source of fascination and delight. When I stumbled upon my first "antiques stall" by accident it was a damascene moment. The range of items you can find is mindboggling, every conceivable object made throughout history in every medium possible. Some things were simply done for the poorest but are now made precious by lustrous surfaces acquired only through hundreds of years' use, and at the other end of the spectrum are objects for kings, jewel-encrusted and created from the most precious materials on Earth to form a container for a few simple grains of salt, or a plate for a roasted chicken leg. No one can fail to be awed by the history, beauty and skill found in these objects and that is at the heart of what drives everyone in this business, with the possible exception of a few miserable, greedy people who sell tat.

'If you ask anyone in antiques, they will give you the same sort of advice: look through lots of sales and auctions and read as many books as you can on the subject that you're interested in before you buy – and that's all very sound advice. Experience has shown me that there are only ever a few very good antiques on the market at any one time and they go fast, be it with a dealer or at an auction. If you find a rare object which you love, a piece you really fall head over heels for, then you should just go for it. An elderly dealer said to me in my early years, "Michael, you should just break yourself to get it, no matter what it costs." That's hard advice to take when you've only ten pounds in your pocket but it's true. You'll often only get one chance to buy that special item and the pieces you remember all your life are the ones that got away.

'Spoons are a great love of mine so I'd be remiss not to offer a few tips should you want to buy them. Remember, nearly all flatware, spoons, forks etc., were made to be used, and used often. Expect some amount of wear, often to the tip or edge of the bowl, or where years of handling around the stem has worn the marks; beware of bowls which are thin or sharp to the edge, showing that a silversmith has reworked a poor condition piece. It might also be the case that a spoon bowl was so worn that a new one is soldered on. In that case, look carefully along the bottom of the stem for any signs of a solder line. To help when looking at any silver or small antique, spending a few pounds on a ten-times-magnification eyeglass will help save you from making expensive mistakes.

'When pieces were sold by good families who had had their crest or arms engraved on the stem, these would be erased (polished off); this can sometimes leave a dish-shaped area at the end of a handle, which may be concealed by later engraving. This is often well done so shouldn't put you off buying an otherwise nice spoon (it is part of its legitimate history), but it should be reflected in the asking price. Fine original engraving on any piece of antique silver always adds to its desirability and value.

'If you're brave but on a budget and want to collect early spoons such as Trefid or Seal Top examples, which can be many thousands if not tens of thousands of pounds, one good tip is to consider buying examples where the marks still haven't been attributed to a particular town or maker. These often achieve much lower prices at auction and are still beautiful examples of the silversmith's work. With research into the history of hallmarks constantly ongoing, you might find that, when a positive attribution of a particular family of hallmarks is made, a hitherto "unascribed" early spoon in your collection will become dramatically more sought-after and valuable as a result, but that should just be considered a bonus not your main aim!

'Whatever you buy, don't buy it as an investment, don't buy it because it's fashionable in design magazines and on TV shows. Just buy objects that *you* find beautiful despite what anyone else thinks – and have some fun buying them, too. Remember that antiques are the well-made survivors of the past and, properly cared for, they'll last not just you for your lifetime, but become heirlooms for generations to come.'

Figure 1 shows three Georgian spoon bowls. To the far left is a spoon in almost pristine condition, with the original thick edge to the lip of the bowl

(these often taper to a point, more so on Continental examples). The centre spoon has a good bowl, with only very slight wear that doesn't affect the shape of the spoon bowl, what you would hope to find on a good eighteenth-century example. The spoon to the right has had wear to the tip of the bowl making it look slightly lopsided. As this wear gets worse, you will find the thin silver at the edge begins to curl over itself, so, if you run your thumbnail lightly over it, it will 'click'.

Figure 2 shows what can be done to a spoon with a worn bowl. This looks free of wear and is not misshapen, but the overall shape of the spoon bowl is wrong to the well-educated eye, much wider and broader at the tip than it should be.

Fig. 1

Fig. 2

PIETRA DURA

So now let's talk about 'hard rock'. No, I haven't gone mad and I'm not about to start raving about rock bands like Black Sabbath or Guns N' Roses, you will no doubt be relieved to hear. 'Hard rock' in Italian is Pietra Dura which is far more of a delight to the eye than it is music to make your ears bleed. Pietra Dura, sometimes referred to as specimen art, was developed from techniques used in ancient Rome to create fabulously tiled mosaic floors and wall decorations. Pietra Dura, however, is a good deal more sophisticated and produces breathtaking works of art.

In a mosaic, small pieces of tile or stone, all basically the same size and shape, are cemented in place, the different colours forming a designed pattern or an image – mathematical tessellations, stylised pictures of animals or gods and even lifelike portraits of real people were produced in mosaic. Pietra Dura is different in the way that the elements of the design or image are inlaid on a stone – usually marble – base. They aren't cemented in place like a mosaic as there is no 'grouting' between the different pieces of coloured stone that make up the design. Each piece of stone, sometimes semi-precious stones or even gemstones, but more often different colours of marble, is cut and carved to a precise shape by the craftsman, then polished and glued in place, butting up so tightly against its neighbours that it is difficult to see the join. Grooves carved into the underside of the inlaid stones hold them together a bit like a kind of jigsaw puzzle and a frame of wood or marble holds everything firmly in place. For the ancient Romans, mosaics were far easier to produce and probably easier to maintain when used as flooring, although small elements of Pietra Dura carved stone are to be found in many mosaics, often as the centrepiece of the design. In Italian, in fact, Pietra Dura is a term that can be used to describe almost any kind of stone carving, but when it is used in English, it refers to this intricate form of inlaid stonework.

Pietra Dura went out of fashion for a while, but by the sixteenth century it was all the rage again with the techniques for the production of the inlay developed and refined as Florence grew to become the centre of production. But what were they producing? Table tops were a popular way of displaying Pietra Dura and were

An example of Pietra Dura in religious decor.

known as specimen tables, a hotchpotch of colours somehow worked together to create wonderful geometric patterns, pictures of ruins, saints or flowers, sometimes mixing vibrant tones with micro mosaic to create an almost three-dimensional image with the seams of the inlaid stones all but invisible. Panels were also produced to decorate church altars or particularly grand items of furniture such as sideboards or cabinets.

Some of these unique works of art probably came into existence as exhibits to show potential customers the standard of workmanship available from a particular craftsman and the different types of stone, particularly white Carrara marble and black or green marble as a base stone, that they could offer.

While the craftsmen were many, the source of the stone was controlled by two powerful families, the Malaspina family, who traced their ownership back to Iacopo Malaspina, the Marquis of Massa who purchased the Lordship of Carrara, from where the stone came, in 1473. Then in 1520 Riciarda Malaspina married Lorenzo Cybo who was born in Sampierdarena, now part of the port area of Genoa. Lorenzo was the son of Franceschetto Cybo, the illegitimate son of Pope Innocent VIII, who, it would seem, was not so innocent after all. Lorenzo's mother was Maddalena de' Medici, whose father, Lorenzo de' Medici, known as *Il Magnifico* ('The Magnificent', if you hadn't already guessed), was the fabulously wealthy ruler of the Florentine Republic, a hugely influential statesman and the sponsor of artists such as Botticelli and Michelangelo. Maddalena's brother became Pope Leo X in 1513.

So what does all that prove? Well, only that the Malaspino-Cybo family was one of the most powerful dynasties in Italy, and one of the things that they controlled was the production of marble, principally from Carrara. They regulated the supply of marble for many years, exporting it all over the world. Marble Arch, now sited at the top of Oxford Street in London but once the ceremonial grand entrance

to Buckingham Palace, is faced with Carrara Marble.

Yet Carrara itself was not the only source of marble. Pietra Dura artists supplemented this delicately veined white or blue-grey marble with other coloured marbles such as the yellow marble from Siena with violet, red, blue or white veins. Essentially, much of the Apuan mountains in Tuscany, with Florence as the region's capital, are marble, but other types of stone were imported from far afield. Pure white marble came from Greek mines in places like Thassos and Naxos, onyx came all the way from Egypt and what is now the Czech Republic, jasper came from Romania and alabaster also came from Egypt.

If you visit Rome, you'll see an extraordinary array of marble in a plethora of situations, often ecclesiastical, sometimes noble, but always sublime. What fascinates me is that these wonderful and extravagant inlays were undertaken in a very hands-on way, let into a base marble using little more than a chisel. It was labour-intensive, but then labour was cheap and although materials were expensive, in mother Italy, known for its coloured stones, at least everything was relatively accessible. Can you imagine a young English gentleman seeing all of this on his 'Grand Tour' (more of which later) and the effort it must have taken to import pieces intact? It would have to have been

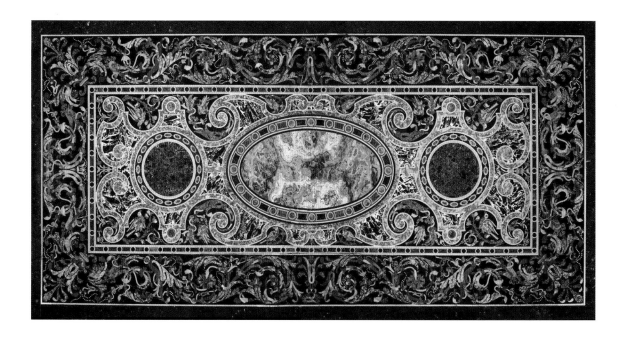

driven by horse and cart to Genoa where it would have been loaded onto a sailing ship and probably, on reaching England, have been reloaded onto a barge for transport by canal and hauled on another cart towed by shire horses through miles of rutted country lanes before being erected using timber scaffolding (for a large panel) and bare-handed brute force?

By the Regency period, the call for specimen tables was so great that faux or pretend tables were being made by hugely reputable craftsmen, who cheated a bit. Instead of using differently coloured stone to create their designs, they used cheaper stone and the different colours were painted on with immense skill. If you're unsure whether it's painted or the real thing, there's one way of deciding and that is the weight! Pietra Dura is incredibly heavy and is also quite cold to touch and simply exudes a glamorous style that, once you have seen and touched the real thing, is simply unmistakable. It still commands good sale room prices today.

Panels of Pietra Dura are available for around £5,000–£10,000, with exceptional and elaborate pieces valued much, much higher. An eighteenth-century specimen and giltwood table will set you back in excess of £50,000.

By the late eighteenth century, specimen tables (a term that can also be used in reference to tables created using inlaid patterns of different colours and types of wood) were being made in Ireland, using Irish stones, and a good Irish piece today will set you back many thousands of pounds. A sixteenth-century Florentine specimen table recently sold at Sotheby's for just shy of £1,000,000 which is an awful lots of noughts!

Do look out for Indian copies, they are pretty but are more often quite matt and don't command the prices of the originals; recently Indian copies were turning up in the trade for as little as £195 while the real thing of course can value into the thousands. That said, Parchin Kari work is a type of specimen construction that comes from India and it has just as much quality and finesse. Examples of Pietra Dura had been exported as widely as India and China since the early seventeenth century and local craftsmen were quick to pick up the techniques, although Parchin Kari tends to use designs, patterns and images that are patently more Indian in character. These became very popular as imports to Britain during the days of the Raj. The finest Parchin Kari work is, of course, to be seen in India, most notable in the Taj

One of the world's most iconic buildings, the Taj Mahal's Pietra Dura is second to none.

Mahal. When this grand mausoleum – a tribute to the love of Shah Jahan for his wife Mumtaz Mahal, who died giving birth to their fourteenth child – was being built between 1632 and 1643, Parchin Kari was a tremendously fashionable, incredibly modern way to add decorative flourishes to a building. In places the white marble was inlaid with lapis lazuli, carnelian, agate and garnet to create designs featuring images of Indian fruits and flowers. That's just one of the reasons why the Taj Mahal is one of the world's most iconic buildings.

As if to add to the truly international flavour of Pietra Dura, talented masons like late eighteenth and early nineteenth century craftsman Giacomo Raffaelli were using stone from as far away as Scotland, China and Siberia. An exceptional piece created by Giacomo is on display in Syon House and I must add that he really is considered the master of micro mosaic and Pietra Dura. A wonderful cabinet made in Rome in 1610 is on display at West Wycombe Park in Buckinghamshire, an amazing country house built as a 'pleasure palace' for the notorious

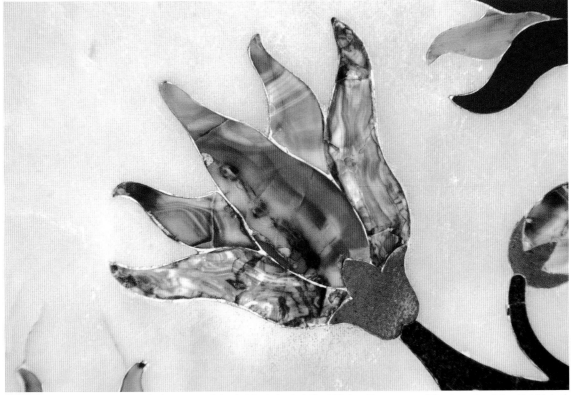

A close-up of the intricately detailed Pietra Dura around the turrets of the Taj Mahal.

hedonist Sir Francis Dashwood. The cabinet was probably purchased by Dashwood in 1740 when he visited Rome. The Dashwood family still lives at West Wycombe House, although the house and grounds are now owned by the National Trust and are open during the summer months. Well worth a visit if you're in the neighbourhood, I'd say. Several extraordinary examples are also on display at Charlecote Park in Warwickshire. Charlecote is a magnificent Victorian mansion, although there has been a manor house on the site for many centuries.

Rumour has it that William Shakespeare was caught poaching in the grounds! Again, it is now a National Trust property and well worth a visit.

As a final note on Pietra Dura, I should say that it is not a technique that died out centuries ago but is still flourishing today, especially with female artisans such as the mother-and-daughter team of Farhana and Meherunnisa Asad in Pakistan, who have created a business employing a number of other talented artists to keep this ancient art very much alive.

INSPIRATION – OSBORNE HOUSE

Britain is a country rich in heritage, and, in my job as a TV presenter, I have been enormously privileged to be able to experience a great deal of our heritage in architecture, design, art, furniture and a multitude of beautiful objects thanks to our surviving stately homes. Wherever you live in Britain, you can be pretty sure that there is a grand house not too far away and, whether they are open to the public as private commercial enterprises, or whether they are run by the likes of English Heritage or the National Trust, we are all lucky to be able to experience some of our nation's history first-hand. One of the perks of my job is that I can sometimes wangle a personal guided tour and I have invariably found that there is great inspiration to be drawn from the taste and style of those who once inhabited – or even still inhabit – the country's magnificent stately homes.

One place that I found particularly inspiring was Osborne House, situated in the quiet and picturesque landscape of the Isle of Wight. The island was a favourite holiday destination for Queen Victoria during her childhood and, in 1845, it became her own family's hideaway home. During one season of *Flog It!* I was able to visit Osborne House and discover what it was about the place that so captivated Queen Victoria and Prince Albert.

On approaching the house, the first things that caught my eye were the twin Italian Renaissance-style towers, one an observation tower and the other housing a magnificent, four-faced clock. I was fortunate enough to be able to climb into the clock tower during my visit but soon found it was no place for royalty – the entrance was through a cupboard door! As I later discovered, the observation tower offered incredible views of the garden and wide, open clearing that stretches right down to the coast. It turned out that Osborne's grounds hadn't always been so accommodating. Prince Albert put his knowledge of forestry and landscaping to good use in designing the avenue through the forest that opens up the view of the sea. All of the trees that stood in the half-mile distance between the front of the house and the ocean were cut down and cleared away. In the days before bulldozers, power tools and the ferocious 'stump grinder' machines that chew up tree stumps, this would have been a massive undertaking. But it did the job; the sweeping views it created are reminiscent of the Bay of Naples, which is just what the prince had in mind.

The royal couple paid for much of the work undertaken at Osborne House through the sale of the Royal Pavilion in Brighton to the local council in 1850. The Royal Pavilion is the famously eccentric palace built for the Prince of Wales, later King George IV, in 1787, although most of what we see today are the extensions and embellishments in an Indian/Islamic style designed and built by John Nash between 1815 and 1822. The palace was also used as a holiday home by George IV's successor, King William IV, who was Queen Victoria's uncle. William IV had no legitimate heirs (although he had no fewer than ten children with the actress

Dorothea Bland, with whom he lived for more than twenty years) so, when he died in 1837, the throne passed to his niece, Victoria. Queen Victoria was not a huge fan of the Royal Pavilion, regarding it as too small for her growing family (she and Prince Albert had nine children) and lacking in privacy.

Brighton had simply become too busy in the summer months, especially at weekends. Steamships for day trippers and the new railways had brought coastal resorts such as Brighton within easy reach of London, opening them up to hordes of tourists.

Previously, the journey would have taken an age in a hugely uncomfortable horse-drawn coach, bumping along over rutted roads and tracks – very expensive and not an ordeal that most people would care to endure for a few hours at the seaside. Steamships docking at piers stretching out into the sea, and the even more popular steam trains, cut the travelling time, avoided the bone-jarring roads and were cheap enough to make the journey affordable. People flocked to the coast, which was great for the prosperity of such seaside towns as Brighton, but not

An engraving of the Royal Pavilion in Brighton from 1842, just a few years before it was sold to the town.

so great if you wanted to get away from the crowds. The Queen wanted a holiday home where she and her family could relax, isolated from the stresses of court life and the prying eyes of gawping tourists. Having spent some happy childhood holidays on the Isle of Wight when her mother, the Duchess of Kent, rented Norris Castle, a stately home on an estate in East Cowes, Queen Victoria and her husband decided to buy the estate next door to Norris – Osborne House – in 1845.

Prince Albert was a great innovator, full of ideas that he had picked up not only from his childhood home in Germany but from his studies in Brussels and Bonn as well as his travels throughout Europe. When the Queen and Prince Albert bought Osborne House for £28,000 from Lady Isabella Blachford, whose family had owned the estate since 1705, the mansion house on the site was deemed too small. It was decided that this should be demolished to make way for a grander residence fit for the royal family. Prince Albert designed the new house in a radical, Italian style, enlisting the help of master builder Thomas Cubitt, who had built many of the most elegant houses in

Belgravia and Pimlico in London, as well as the new front elevation of Buckingham Palace. Osborne House took shape between 1845 and 1851, although the final part of the building was not added until forty years later.

The royal family spent a great deal of time at Osborne House, especially during the spring and summer. At the end of the avenue, through the trees there is a small beach, which was their private bathing beach. There the Queen had her own bathing machine – one of those peculiar sheds on wheels that would trundle into the water with ladies on board so that they could then walk down a set of steps into the sea without the indignity of being seen struggling on that awkward bit between the sand and the deeper water. It was also for privacy, of course, but they went in for a 'swim' – more of a bob around for ladies – wearing almost as much as they did when they sat down to tea. The royals also enjoyed visits to Osborne just before Christmas, although a dip in the Solent probably wasn't on their agenda in chilly December, no matter how much they were wearing!

You will have realised by now, of course, that I absolutely love places like this. Well, what's not to like, really? Places like Osborne

House are there for us to stroll around when we feel like it, sometimes for a small fee, but without all the headaches and the responsibility that come with their upkeep. It is always amazing to walk through the doors of an old house, and, as I made my way out of Osborne's grounds and through the door used by guests and officials, I found myself entering another world. Like so many other houses of its kind, Osborne has a way of taking you back into the past, but there is also something unique about the place. It has an amazingly personal feel, which makes sense when you look at its history. Queen Victoria and Prince Albert were the first and last of the royal family to live at Osborne, and so it contained no hand-me-downs. Everything inside the house had once been theirs, and the furnishings not only reflected their tastes but also provided a rare glimpse into their personal lives.

Walking through the house's ornate sculpture hall, I marvelled at its contents: in amongst the grand works preferred by Prince Albert were the more subtle, sentimental pieces favoured by the Queen.

Queen Victoria's personal bathing machine, which went on public display at Osborne House for the first time in 2012.

131

My favourite of these was a statue of Noble, Queen Victoria's much-loved collie. In the drawing room, however, it was Prince Albert's choice of furnishings that took centre stage. A pair of pedestal chandeliers by Ostlers of Birmingham, the creation of which was overseen by the prince himself, sat below three equally impressive chandeliers that were hanging from the ceiling and the whole room flowed together with elegance and grandeur. Indeed, Queen Victoria herself once labelled the room as 'handsome'.

But it was the couple's private quarters that really told their story. The sitting room looked lived in, by no means messy, but distinctly more cluttered than the rest of the house. Two writing desks sat side by side, indicating just how much of their time the couple had spent together, and there was even evidence that the children had once been allowed to play here, a very unusual occurrence for royalty during the 1800s. It seemed as if life at the house had been idyllic, and that is surely what drew them back to Osborne whenever they had the chance.

Then, in December 1861, Prince Albert died at Windsor Castle at the age of just forty-two. There are conflicting theories

The drawing room at Osborne House.

about the cause of his death, but he had been suffering from persistent stomach trouble, although he maintained a heavy workload, including ongoing developments at Osborne House. Reports indicate that, all at once, this family home became a retreat and a place of mourning. As one stepped into the master bedroom, this was very obvious. It is said that Queen Victoria never quite recovered from Prince Albert's death, and, even as she lived out her final days many years later, the portrait she kept of him remained on her bedside table. On the headboard of the bed I could see a small plaque detailing the first

and the last time the couple had spent the night here together.

Queen Victoria was devastated by the death of Prince Albert and withdrew into an extended period of mourning that led some to question whether she had lost her mind. She shunned London, spending more time at Osborne or, even farther away, at Balmoral in Scotland. Eventually she was persuaded to return to public life, although she wore only black for the rest of her life. As she had done every year since Prince Albert's death, the Queen spent Christmas of 1900 at Osborne House. She had become increasingly unwell

The Durbar room, designed by Lockwood Kipling and completed in 1892, reflected the Queen's love of India and status as its Empress.

over the preceding months and she died at Osborne on 22 January 1901.

Osborne House was the private property of the royal family, much as Sandringham or Balmoral is today, and Queen Victoria had stated in her will that she wanted the estate to remain within the family. Sadly, Osborne held few charms for the Queen's surviving children and none of them wanted to take on the expense of maintaining the house and grounds. So, on the day of his coronation, 9 August 1902, King Edward VII presented the house to the nation. Instead of a royal retreat, it became a Royal Navy training school and a convalescent home for army officers, although the rooms used by Queen Victoria and Prince Albert were sealed, not opened to the public until 1954. Since 1986, Osborne House has been run by English Heritage and millions have been spent on preserving and restoring the house and grounds in order to allow all of us an intimate glimpse into the life of one of our most celebrated monarchs.

Inside Queen Victoria and Prince Albert's bedroom at Osborne House, the room in which the Queen died on 22 January 1901.

POP ART

Pop art was born of post-war austerity. Colourful, vigorous, brash, ironic and fun, it gave artists the freedom to express themselves in ways that hadn't been seen since the Impressionists in the nineteenth century and, to a lesser degree, the art-deco movement in the 1920s. In some ways, pop art nods towards Dalí and Mondrian, while others might say that the political posters of Stalinist Russia, with their distinctive use of primary colours and overprinted borders, sowed the seeds of this art form.

But pop art is also its own genre, sitting firmly at the head of the counterculture vanguard and crying out for us to think about the world around us. By using consumer culture to deliver a message about the way we live in our modern world, pop art challenges the values of our society. How does it do that? Well, think of the multilayered images of Marilyn Monroe by Andy Warhol or his famous *Campbell's Soup Cans*. The publicity photograph of Marilyn Monroe on which Warhol based his series of multicoloured and black-and-white images was taken in the 1950s, but Warhol created his piece shortly after her death in 1962. The repeat images show how

overexposed she was as a celebrity – an instantly recognisable image, no matter how it was treated, ultimately fading away just as she did. Yet the bright, vibrant colours are also fun and funny, reflecting something of her personality – maybe. You can pin as many interpretations on the work as you like, really, which is all part of the appeal of pop art.

And the soup cans? Another colourful, fun image, using an icon of consumerism to poke fun at consumerism. Repeated images of something that you see on a supermarket shelf shouldn't be art, should it? That's what you're expected to think at first. It's a bit of a shock, but then you smile because it's also quite amusing and the art has done its job by making you think.

The history books tell us over and over again that pop art started life in early-1950s Britain partly as a response to American consumerism that had raised its head in Britain during the Second World War. American troops stationed in the UK, were seen as 'oversexed, overpaid and over here' – a much-used phrase but, a bit like pop art, it expresses a popular feeling with some humour. Many Brits were jealous

A 1983 piece, 'Painting with Statue of Liberty', by Roy Lichtenstein, one of the most famous pop artists, on display at the Smithsonian National Gallery of Art in Washington, DC.

of the Americans, who appeared to have easy access to luxury items that were not readily available in wartime Britain. Pop art was a reaction to American appetites and overindulgence. So let's get this straight: pop art is an ironic, subversive tool that manipulates our perceptions and pokes fun at the established order, but it is also used as a selling tool by multinational corporations who, even more ironically, are a major part of the establishment that fostered this new creed of artist in the first place! The fact is that pop art, in all its different forms, has produced some fantastic pieces that, love them or hate them, are difficult to ignore.

Personally, I think there is far more to love than to hate.

Although pop art first began to emerge in the 1950s, it's not too difficult to find earlier work that can be described as pre-empting the movement. Three American artists, Gerald Murphy, Stuart Davis and Charles Demuth, created paintings in the 1920s that contained imagery from American commercial products and advertising designs, as did the 1940s collages of Scottish artist and sculptor Eduardo Paolozzi. He became Sir Eduardo in 1989 and sadly passed away in 2005, but we will hear more of him shortly. So, the roots of pop art may stretch back further into the past than we first realise, but it is also reaching forward into the future: there are ongoing dialogues in Internet chatrooms and the art media about whether street art should be seen as part of the pop-art movement, or regarded as a different genre altogether.

When we think of pop art I guess most people instinctively think of Andy Warhol, yet Britain boasts a proud heritage of pop-art genius that owes its development to the RCA, or Royal College of Art. The RCA started life in 1836 as the Government School for Design and, by 1851, it had become the National Art Training School. It wasn't until 1896 that it finally became the RCA and it has since fostered the talents of wonderfully creative people from Christopher Dresser and Edward Lutyens to Gertrude Jekyll and Kate Greenaway, known for her children's book illustrations. More recent alumni include James Dyson, Zandra Rhodes, Tracey Emin, musician Ian Dury and brothers Tony and Ridley Scott.

In 2008, the artist Sir Peter Blake, who also studied at the RCA, kindly invited me to an art exhibition and I jumped at the opportunity to meet this wonderful gentleman, who remains one of my pop-art heroes. His notable artworks include subjects as famous as Elvis and the Beatles – he designed the iconic *Sgt. Pepper* album cover. He was a forerunner of the pop-art movement as championed by the likes of David Hockney and indeed exhibited alongside Hockney and American artist

Ronald Brooks Kitaj in 1961 at the RCA's Young Contemporaries exhibition. By 1963 David was being represented in swinging London by Robert Fraser, who was affectionately known as Groovy Bob. Robert

Warhol was savvy; Hockney, too, was ever creative yet responding to our subconscious through the mood of an era. Who hasn't been seduced by product placement? It has to be mentioned that Warhol and Hockney

From the 2013 'Pop Art Design' exhibition at the Barbican in London, which brought together works by a range of artists and designers including Peter Blake, Richard Hamilton, Andy Warhol, and Claes Oldenburg.

– or, as I prefer, Groovy Bob – was primarily an art dealer with a gallery he called 'the shop' in Duke Street, London, but the way he embraced and exhibited cool work by cool artists made him a favourite of the Beatles and Rolling Stones and brought him into contact with creative photographers such as David Bailey.

also gave expression to their sexuality at a time when society still criminalised homosexuality. While some composers and singers were writing songs that furtively helped bring about the social changes that we take for granted today, Hockney and Warhol bravely created art – such as Hockney's *We Two Boys Together Clinging*,

'Refreshing and Delicious', 1949, was one of Eduardo Paolozzi's works that signalled the beginning of the Pop Art movement.
© *Trustees of the Paolozzi Foundation, Licensed by DACS 2018.*

painted in 1961, when he was in his second year at the RCA – that placed them at the forefront of media scrutiny. Surrealism, yes, but with a message.

As the 1960s progressed, there came a new era of sexual liberation and acceptance, with fashions and styles that challenged and titillated, and ultimately the summer of peace and love. Hippy flower power would give way to the 'glam rock' era in the seventies, but pop art was here to stay. It wasn't hidden, it was out and proud and, if the established order disliked it, youth embraced it. Pop art made its mark, influencing the baby-boom generation and becoming a catalyst for everything from punk to hip-hop, political posters and street art.

In an interview in *The Guardian* in 2006, Sir Peter Blake (he became Sir Peter in 2002) spoke about his work: 'I wanted to make an art that was the visual equivalent of pop music. When I made a portrait of Elvis I was hoping for an audience of 16-year-old girl Elvis fans, although that never really worked.' Peter goes on to state that he's asked about *Sgt. Pepper* in every interview and that he was initially paid only £200 for the artwork. Well, I'm guilty of mentioning the Beatles: I'm one of those interviewers. Sorry, Peter! It's just that I love your work.

Peter incorporated a gnome into the *Sgt.*

Pepper album, which recently sold in New York for $42,000 – and that's part of the quirkiness that I adore about this art form. I love the vibrancy and colour, the messages and the *hidden* messages. Pop art is like one of those places you visit, like Avebury with its magnificent megaliths and the huge ditch – more than five thousand years of history, yet whoever created it all those years ago knew exactly how to multi-please. You see, Avebury works on so many levels. You can theorise about it, embrace it, worship within its space, have some quiet time, let the kids run themselves out of energy time, a picnic. The space is whatever you want it to be. And that is exactly how I would describe my passion for pop art. Whether it's a Hockney or a Blake, you are immediately touched in some unique way by the art and, whether it's the way my kids latch onto the vibrancy, or the way I delve into the hidden messages, it's all summed up in the sense that we are all fans of something. No one has the right to intellectualise appreciation of art and no one has the right to belittle others for the creativity that attracts them. Other art may sometimes be guilty of intellectualising and marginalising, but I defy you to say that about pop art.

Sir Peter Blake is my hero and, I'll be honest, when I met him it was the only time in my life that I've asked a celebrity for a selfie. He really is the Godfather of pop art. While it has been reported that Peter received a settlement for his *Sgt. Pepper* album cover, and he's recently produced another cover for Eric Clapton, I understand how he feels about being constantly referred to as 'the artist who did the *Sgt. Pepper* cover'. I know a bit about what it is like to be pigeonholed for one aspect of your life. Wherever I go, I get so many lovely people approach me to say how much they love *Flog It!*. They may talk of how their nan or their uncle collects Clarice Cliff or football programmes; they may say how much they like one of the experts. But they all want to talk about one thing: the show! So I get it. I've lived a full and fortunate life; I've experienced the same highs and lows as most people do; I've had other careers and I'm blessed with two lovely children and a wife I love dearly too. But my public persona means that one thing is referred to again and again: *Flog It!*. 'Hello, Mr *Flog It!*.' I hope you get what I mean. It's generally meant in good spirit and with affection for a show millions of people watch every week. They enjoy the show in the way that people *love* the *Sgt. Pepper* art, and I

do hope that the album cover serves as an introduction to the many, many other works of art that Peter has created.

Perhaps that album cover may also help people to think about exploring the other artists and sculptors, musicians and writers that pop art encompasses. So check out Peter's other work – my personal favourites include *The Beach Boys* and his portrait of David Hockney. I'd also add that Peter is for ever developing ideas and I remember seeing an interview with him in which he talked about collages and his flatmate who taught him that collages didn't need to include a bus ticket, as he thought they always had a bus ticket in them! Peter also says the act of collecting is a conceptual art form and, if I could champion one statement by this behemoth of pop art, it would be that. All antique dealers and every collector will empathise with those words.

Still not sure what pop art really is? Well, maybe this will help. In a letter to his two architect friends Peter and Alison Smithson in 1957, artist Richard Hamilton described pop art thus: 'Popular (designed for a mass audience), Transient (short-term solution), Expendable (easily forgotten), Low cost, Mass produced, Young (aimed at youth), Witty, Sexy, Gimmicky, Glamorous, Big business.'

Today I would add it's something to collect and enjoy, whatever your age. And, in the words of Peter, remember that your collection and how you display it makes yours a 'conceptual art form' of its own. My mum and dad had Zandra Rhodes designs in the house, specifically a bed headboard and soft furnishings, typical of the period. I expect many of you grew up with her designs, too. In a cluttered family home, these items were lovely homely comforts but probably a bit lost. The space around an item gives it a sense of importance; it draws the eye in. If you're selling items, display them like this whether in an antique shop or an online auction, or even at a boot sale – you'll get more money!

Nowadays, pop art has become a must-have of mainstream culture with a million fridge magnets and postcards demonstrating that pop culture has become mainstream in the psyche of millions. Yet there is still so much original work out there and plenty of scope to discover new artists. If ever you meet an artist, ask them to do a doodle and sign it! The worst that can happen is that they can only say no. Peter drew a rocket for my son Dylan, as Dylan had sent him a collage. He also signed and did some doodles for me on a *Flog It!* script. Those are things that Dylan and I will always treasure.

Pop art was last explored in depth in the UK in 1991 with an exhibition at the Royal

Yoko Honda's 'Lemonwater Love', 2015, is an example of Pop Art's continuing development in the twenty-first century.

Academy, yet many auction houses hold pop art sales a couple of times a year. Dreweatts and Sotheby's have set auction records for Andy Warhol's *Madonna and Self-Portrait with Skeleton Arm (after Munch)* and Richard Hamilton's *My Marilyn*, while Christie's held the influential 'When Britain Went Pop' sale in 2013. It's a blossoming genre for collectors because there are examples by overlooked artists, whose work is exceptional, turning up in provincial auction rooms where their work sits uncomfortably among the kind of brown furniture and Royal Doulton one might expect at such sales. Dealers such as Drew Pritchard mix graffiti panels and pop art among their otherwise more traditional stock, while London galleries such as Stolen Space, Pictures On Walls and Lazarides offer collectors street art in its deepest sense.

We have come across lots of items of pop art on *Flog It!*. We saw lots of comics when we visited Dundee in Scotland, where DC

Thomson produced *The Dandy* and *The Beano*, along with loads of other classic comics. An original copy of the very first *Dandy* (1937) or *Beano* (1938) would be expected to fetch over £20,000 at auction, but it was a little further south where we found one of my favourite pieces. When *Flog It!* visited the Our Dynamic Earth centre in Edinburgh, I met a gentleman called Bill who had brought along an heirloom that had spent the last thirty-one years in his attic – a plastic elephant.

In 1972 Nairn Floors, a company based in Fife, where linoleum was a traditional industry, decided that it needed to make architects more aware of their flooring products. It commissioned the eminent artist and sculptor Eduardo Paolozzi (told you we would get back to Eduardo eventually!) to design its elephant. When I first saw an image of this sculpture, I thought it was made of cut-up sheets of lino, glued on top of one another, but, slightly oddly (to my mind), it's made from plastic. The sculptor worked with a plastics engineer, Keith Powell, to develop a way of casting from a wood-wax mould. Not only did it have to stand up straight and convey strength, intelligence and rugged beauty, but the elephant also had to conceal a 10-inch × 8-inch box, for product literature. The literature was specially designed, too, involving leading illustrators and architectural photographer Phil Sayer, who shoots 'Me and My House' for *C20* magazine.

There were originally 3,000 of these elephants, all numbered. I wonder how many have survived? Back in 1973 *Design Journal* commented, 'It's hoped that architects will treasure them, hoard them – anything except throw them away unopened along with the other trade samples.' Bill's elephant had been used to store household bills, mail and suchlike, sitting on a sideboard for a time. They used to pick it up by the trunk to move it about but, when the trunk broke, the elephant was banished to the attic. When buying pop art, condition is all important, as it is with so many antiques, so, despite this being an important work of pop art (they have one at the Victoria and Albert Museum in London), when we took it to the Thomson Roddick Auction Rooms in Rosewell just south of Edinburgh, it had an estimate of £200-£300. Auctioneer Sybelle Thomson eventually brought the hammer down at £950! Bill, of course, was delighted and pop art had certainly brought a smile to the face of one happy *Flog It!* viewer.

'El Cap de Barcelona' ('The Head of Barcelona'), a sculpture created by Lichtenstein for the 1992 Summer Olympics that incorporates pop art and Barcelona's own artistic heritage in the use of ceramic tile.

STUDIO POTTERY

Around the time that pop art was establishing itself, studio pottery was beginning to pick up in popularity. Names that we know today such as Troika (founded in St Ives, Cornwall, in the early 1960s), stars of the genre such as Austrian ceramicist Lucie Rie, and lesser-known, yet just as artistic, talents such as Clive Brooker were just finding their feet sixty years ago, but studio pottery is actually far older than that. In introducing you to this genre – and, believe me, it is a genre – I need to explain a little about its background. We are all used to traditional names such as Royal Doulton, Meissen and Wedgewood (did you know that sometimes its pottery was marked 'Wadgewood'?) making good money at auction, but, at the end of the Second World War, the art world reached a strange crossroads: one fork sired modernistic art-house pottery, the other returned to more traditional methods. Studio pottery involved the potters – the artists – in every aspect of the production of their work, creating the piece from a lump of clay, the design and decoration and firing it in their own kiln.

Studio pottery has its roots in early-twentieth-century design, taking its influence from traditional tea bowls and Stone Age pots as well as the Art Nouveau ceramics of the Ruskin Pottery studio, and the Arts and Crafts movement's Liberty ware. There is also a nod towards seventeenth-century slipware. Following the despicable horrors of the Second World War, the world of art and design turned away from the naturalistic, purely because Nazism and Japanese imperialism had perverted everything natural and ancient using such styles to promote the dogma of their own ideology. As the world became aware of the evils that the Axis Powers had inflicted on those they conquered, anything with a uniquely naturalistic, Germanic, Japanese or even pagan identity was, to a degree, shunned. It wasn't until the 1960s, when 'Peace and Love' became the buzz words of the hippy culture, that people once again looked at Neolithic stone circles, primitive shapes and nature for inspiration. The hippy 'flower power'

A couple of examples of Studio Pottery's influences: a Neolithic vase from the Fontbouisse culture (the modern-day Languedoc region in southern France) , dated 2300-1700 BC (left), and a piece of seventeenth century slipware by Thomas Toft (right).

movement started in America in the 1960s, a youth movement that spawned liberal philosophies of anti-war sentiment, the desire to decriminalise drugs, indulge in free love and shun mainstream political ideology. It also embraced Eastern mysticism and paganism, popularising the works of Aleister Crowley, William Blake and Madame Blavatsky.

This counterculture grew from the beatnik generation and attracted a broad-based following of political activists, protesting against the war in Vietnam and the proliferation of nuclear weapons, among other things. They inspired some of the best-loved, most evocative songs of the period: 'San Francisco (Be Sure to Wear Flowers in Your Hair)' by Scott McKenzie, 'People Got to Be Free' by the Rascals, Jefferson Airplane's 'Somebody to Love' and, of course, 'All You Need Is Love' by the Beatles. I am reminded of my visit to the ISKCON (International Society for Krishna Consciousness) temple at Letchmore Heath near Watford in Hertfordshire a few years ago, where

I interviewed Gouri Das, the temple president. His spiritual path had taken him from punk rock, through a spiritual awakening, to ISKCON's Bhaktivedanta Manor, formerly Piggots Manor of Letchmore Heath. George Harrison bought the manor house and the estate for ISKCON in 1973 and it was renamed after the society's founder. It was here that Gouri Das embraced Eastern mysticism and religion as an escape from the fragilities he saw in the modern world.

So how does studio pottery fit into this picture, seeing that it had already been around for the best part of sixty years by the time the hippy counterculture came along? Well, by the 1960s, studio pottery had simply come of age! The new attitudes of the swinging sixties brought those influences that had fallen out of favour after WWII back into vogue, shaking off their Nazi connotations.

Ironically, the vanguard of studio pottery was led by a potter named Hans Coper, who had been born into the turbulent world of 1920s Germany in a city called Chemnitz in Saxony, which later became part of East Germany during the communist years.

Like many Germans, Hans was appalled by the rise of Nazism and all it peddled, fleeing Germany in 1939 only to arrive in a Britain, where he was instantly held as an enemy alien. Having been interned, he was sent to Canada until 1942, when he was allowed to return to England. As a conscientious objector, he served in the non-combatant corps until the end of the war. In 1946, with no experience of ceramics, Hans was hired by Lucie Rie, working in London. Lucie made ceramic buttons in her studio at 18 Albion Mews, which she leased through the Church Commissioners' Hyde Park Estate. If you go there today, you'll see a blue plaque in Lucie's memory. She lived there until her death on 1 April 1995.

Although Hans had no ceramic experience, Lucie's Jewish roots and Hans's abhorrence of Nazism gave them something in common in postwar London, and, besides, Lucie needed someone to help her fire all the buttons! Hans was delighted to be offered tea and cake, which Lucie offered to pretty much every visitor, and soon started work helping her. Hans was eager to learn and Lucie sent him to a potter

A selection of Alan and Pat's absolutely extraordinary collection of Hans Coper and Lucie Rie's pottery at their home in West Yorkshire.

called Heber Mathews to learn his trade. Having mastered the basics of the potter's wheel, Hans returned to help Lucie and it's from that time we find lots of cups and saucers made by both Rie and Coper. In 1948, they exhibited together and Coper became a partner in Rie's studio until 1950. They were to remain friends until Hans died in Frome, Somerset, in 1981.

The style of pottery produced by Hans has an almost ethnographic appearance, yet is also reminiscent of the kind of strange alien creations seen in sci-fi films

such as *The Time Machine*. Despite this, you feel almost compelled to pick it up! Now, while our *Flog It!* valuation days often uncover Troika, Bitossi, those huge West German lava lamps and studio glass such as Whitefriars, all of which are hugely collectible, Coper pieces are far more rare. I was intrigued, therefore, when my good friend and *Flog It!* auctioneer Adam Partridge told me that he had a collection of twenty-one pieces of Hans Coper turn up last year, and the tale is extraordinary!

The collection came from the home

of Alan and Pat. Probation officer Alan passed away in 2015 and he had lived in a modest bungalow on the outskirts of Leeds with his dear wife Pat, who had sadly passed away in 2012. Adam referred to them as good, honest, working-class Yorkshire folk, but hidden behind the curtains was forty years of collecting. I suppose, looking back, they did exactly what I'd suggest you do with art and ceramics, and that's find an artist you like, get to know their work and visit their pottery – which is exactly what Alan and Pat had done. If I tell you that the first piece of Hans Coper pottery they bought cost £33, you'll probably think that doesn't sound particularly extravagant. However, when I tell you that this was in 1974 and the average salary was £3,200 a year, you'll think again. I guess that works out at about half a week's wages!

Anyway, the basis of their collection was twenty-one pieces of Coper and fifteen pieces of Rie. I chuckled to hear that four pieces of Coper's work were displayed on top of their TV set, which so reminded me of my mum and dad. Well, the TV set was an item of furniture

when the screen was mounted in a wooden box, so why not use the top as a display shelf? You certainly couldn't do that with today's flat-screen sets. What astounded me most was that these remarkable items had survived sharing their home with two cats! I think you can assume by now that Alan and Pat were serious collectors and, indeed, their collection was known about by aficionados of Coper and Rie. Yet when Alan passed away the beneficiary of the estate, his nephew, at first thought about simply having the house cleared to speed up the sale of the bungalow.

Adam's colleague Jason Wood had taken a call about a collection of studio pottery and instantly knew its significance. This really is the Holy Grail of studio pottery, and thankfully it went under the hammer, rather than someone mallet-clearing everything into a skip. I don't think Jason or Adam, or indeed Alan's nephew, was ready for what happened next. There were a few other studio items in the collection, but the sum and total was an astonishing £861,460.

Coper's story wouldn't be complete without my writing a little more about

Lucie Rie with one of her wonderful pots.

Lucie Rie. Lucie was an extraordinary lady – anyone who makes a cup of tea and offers cake to visitors gets an awful lot of Brownie points in my book! I sometimes indulge myself by looking into the background of artists, cabinetmakers and potters to get a sense of where their genius came from. With Lucie, that's not difficult to see, as her father was Sigmund Freud's consultant and she grew up in that most wonderfully imperial city, Vienna. Traditionally, Vienna was one of the trade hubs of Europe and a real melting pot of cultures, its coffee shops and market places bustling with the life and vigour that also made it a hugely important centre for music and art.

Lucie set up her first studio in Vienna in 1925 and exhibited in 1937 in Paris alongside Picasso, who showed his famous

This Lucie Rie porcelain bowl features some lovely sgraffito detailing, which was hugely fashionable in the 1960s.

painting, *Guernica*, about the horrors of war. Lucie's work received complete acclaim and a silver medal, yet a year later she had to flee Austria for her life when the Nazis seized the country. Lucie moved to London with as much of her collection as she could ship. During the war, the ceramic buttons she made in her spare time, while working in an optical factory by day, drew attention to her creativity and

today they can be seen at the Sainsbury Art Gallery in Norwich as well as at the Victoria and Albert Museum (V&A) in London, where part of her studio has also been reconstructed as a display. Isn't it amazing how something as beautifully small and simple as a button can become a standalone item that you can exhibit?

Lucie is undoubtedly a huge influence on studio potters but what was it that

Lucie Rie and Bernard Leach were close friends as well as pioneers of Studio Pottery.

most influenced her? Well, it's said that in 1940 she visited the newly opened Alexander Keiller Museum in Avebury to gaze at the Neolithic pots. Many of the exhibits dated back to the erection of the stone circles and showed a naïve beauty that mirrored wonderfully Lucie's concept of the perfect pot. Certainly there are just as many cues from Neolithic pottery to the studio pottery we see today as there are from Japanese and Chinese ceramics.

Coper was a godsend for Rie. They shared a commonality of interests and often exhibited together, and I must add that if anyone ever says, 'Studio pottery all looks the same,' they really don't know what they are talking about. Yes, there are strong influences, yes there are sometimes similarities of design, but when you get to know Lucie's work and that of Coper, and look at it alongside pieces from an artist such as Bernard Leach, you'll instantly get a sense of the difference, a sense of their individual dynamic and a sense of their own perceptions of what they feel works best. In 1948 Lucie and Hans Coper took their friend from New York, artist and photographer Stella Snead, to Avebury to look again at the museum pots, the wonderful Neolithic stones and Silbury Hill. When you look at some of Lucie's work from that period you can see the rounded form of Silbury making its presence felt. Lucie rarely commented on her work but did say: 'To make pottery is an adventure to me, every new work is a new beginning. Indeed I shall never cease to be a pupil.' When I look at Lucie's work it becomes apparent that each piece she made is just as important, in her hands and in her mind, as the last one. This is what makes someone like Lucie stand out – nothing she made was pedestrian, ordinary or expected.

Lucie certainly had a brilliant business head, selling her pottery in a series of galleries and shops throughout Britain. She sold in St Ives, Devon, Oxford, Edinburgh and London. Tableware by Rie and Coper – coffee cups, sugar bowls, milk jugs and the like – with dark-brown glaze and finely etched lines known as 'sgraffito', was marketed as the height of design style in upmarket stores such as Heal's. From 1970 onwards her work was exhibited at important galleries in London, including

Here's a Lucie Rie bowl on the left, and a Hans Coper pot on the right. Both really showcase the originality of their work.

the Crafts Council shop at the V&A Museum, and in the King's Road, which, in its ultimate incarnation as the street of cool, was home to the Marjorie Parr Gallery at 285 King's Road. Today it's a shoe shop, nestled alongside Raffles Bar, favoured haunt of the rich and famous, with another über-cool watering hole called JuJu directly opposite.

I don't think Lucie would have cared too much for the glamorous, rock-star lifestyle such establishments exude, although, as a young girl in Austria, she certainly grew up in a privileged world, with all the trappings of wealth. Her family moved in the right circles and she had the confidence some say a private education brings. In an article in *The Guardian* in 2012, journalist Edmund de Waal said of her: 'Even in old age, the potter Lucie Rie, slight, immaculate in white, could be dauntingly rude.' I prefer to use the term 'feisty', because maybe what Edmund missed was that, throughout a life where she had demonstrated so much creative talent, Lucie had been bombarded with the opinions of others, yet she knew exactly what she was and what she could do. That her work pleased others was perhaps incidental to the process. Sure, it sold, but pottery was what she loved. She didn't have children, she had her kiln and wheel, and the community of studio potters could be seen as her family. Lucie's work in my world as a dealer and collector is very special.

Emmanuel Cooper, potter, writer, activist and broadcaster, wrote a book about Lucie and, if you can find a copy, you'll see that it's well worth a read as it gives a fascinating insight into this wonderful artist's world. I don't suppose she would have wanted to be in my book but, given what a huge impact she had on the genre, I couldn't write about studio pottery without writing my own personal homage to Lucie Rie.

The studio pottery movement was a close-knit community and one of Lucie's closest friends was another of my heroes,

Bernard Leach. Bernard Howell Leach was an extraordinary potter born in Hong Kong in 1887. Bernard's father was a colonial judge and, sadly, his mother died in childbirth. Baby Bernard then spent most of his first three years with his maternal grandparents in Japan but, when his father married again, he returned to Hong Kong, eventually moving on to Singapore when his father was transferred there. These formative years are important because of the huge influence that the art and ceramic techniques of the Far East were to have on Bernard's future work.

We'll look at his pottery shortly and when we do you'll be able to see how his studio pottery is full of Eastern influence and the kind of design that fits wonderfully into pretty much any environment, whether a modern city apartment, a suburban 'between-the-wars' semi or a country cottage. If I'm going to be pedantic, it probably looks out of place in a Georgian mansion and, I was going to say, a Victorian villa, but mixing it with Arts and Crafts furniture allows it to take on a sculptural beauty even there. So, like all great potters, Bernard thought

A pot from the Chinese Yang Shao culture – Neolithic pottery was a huge inspiration behind the Studio Pottery movement.

about form and function way beyond the function of an item being, say, a milk jug.

When he was ten, Bernard was sent to school in England and he went on to attend the Slade School of Art in London, as well as the London School of Art in Kensington. While he was in England, he met and fell in love with his cousin, Muriel, and they were married when Bernard moved back to Japan in 1908. I can't believe the amount of globetrotting he did in the age of steam and sail. There was no way to hop on a jet in London in the morning and arrive in Tokyo a few hours later. When Bernard did his travelling, those sorts of journeys took weeks. In Japan he met with Shirakaba-ha, a literary and artistic group that had studied at the Peers School, or the Gakushūin, which was originally created to educate the children of Japan's nobility.

Anxious to learn more about Chinese art, Bernard also worked for a time in Peking, even moving his young family (by 1915 he and Muriel had a son and a daughter) there for a time. I fell in love with China in 2011 when I was filming for the TV series *The Manor Reborn*, which involved the refurbishment of Avebury Manor for the National Trust. Why China? Well, it was a great place to go to commission hand-painted wallpaper and, yes, ceramics. China is such an amazing country and the way it feeds your senses with a never-ending visual feast of designs and styles really sparks my imagination. Imagine actually being there around the time of the Last Emperor? Wow! I guess the nearest most of us will ever get to experiencing that kind of imagery is in the movies, but Bernard truly lived that world and experienced both China and Japan

in a time of extreme change, made all the more bizarre by a comment he made in 1920 that he didn't speak Japanese.

I think it's safe to say that Bernard was well connected and he even published a couple of booklets in Japan to accompany exhibitions of his work. Bernard returned to England, but not before he had put on an acclaimed exhibition in the Japanese city of Osaka, where he caught the eye of Japanese potter Shōji Hamada. When Bernard and his family set sail for England in 1920, Shōji accompanied them.

Let's move on to St Ives – my old stomping ground! Did I tell you that? If you watch *Flog It!* you'll know how much I love Cornwall, and whenever I visit it's like going home. My best childhood memories come from there. With its sandy beaches and amazing light it's easy to see why it has attracted countless artists and potters over the years. Bernard was no exception. He had become tremendous friends with Shōji, so Bernard, Muriel and Shōji travelled to Cornwall, where they set up a studio. Shōji stayed for three years before returning home to Japan.

It's a nice addition to our story to learn

that many famous potters would learn their art under the guidance of Bernard. His friends back in Japan must have been very proud of their Western protégé. Bernard is sometimes called the Father of Studio Pottery, but to me he is the Godfather of Studio Pottery, the pinnacle of creativity. When he passed away in 1979 he left behind an extraordinary legacy and story.

Bernard's pottery comes up in auction every so often and, like most exceptional artists, he went through styles and periods. You can buy small Leach Pottery items for under £50, which is a great way to start a collection. Larger pieces with the Japanese influence much more evident start at around £900. Earthy brown and later glossy glazes, drips and dips and painted figures are what Bernard's pottery is all about. It's organic and tactile and it must have offered a real antidote to the smooth, classical forms most people were used to. The secret of Bernard's success lay not only in his genius of design and use of slip but in the sort of kiln used, too. A round, up-draught kiln was used to fire decorated earthenware and slipware dishes, lead-glazed tableware and the Japanese raku, which is a low-temperature firing, where the pots were often removed from the kiln while the glaze was in a molten form. Rhododendrons and even driftwood were used to fuel the kilns, and Bernard's early firings weren't very successful. Neither he nor Shōji had enough experience of controlling the firing, especially given that they were using such a wide variety of fuel, and thermal shock would destroy the pots. Only a small percentage of the early pots he and Shōji created were a success, but, honestly, success isn't the word. Unique, beautiful, tactile and a host of other adjectives spill into my thoughts. I imagine them laughing away, chucking swept-up floor mess into the kiln, including the dust and detritus, the resulting inexact temperature of the kiln causing the bizarre, almost alien, surface textures. This is what studio pottery is all about.

Bernard continued working until 1972 and, even after his eyesight failed, he wrote books on pottery and in all his years he never lost his love of travelling, making him a truly global artist. He was to marry three times and had a notoriously

Bernard Leach pictured in 1977 at the V&A in London – the Far Eastern influences in his work are on full display here.

tempestuous manner with family and friends, living his own life his own way; yet his pottery remains primarily an expression of emotion that bears testament to his energy and enthusiasm for an art form: studio pottery.

In 1977 the V&A held an exhibition of Bernard Leach's pottery. It's so satisfying to know that such a talented man was celebrated as a great British creative genius within his own lifetime, yet he remains more famous in Japan than in England. To my mind, that bears testament to his status more than anything else. In the cradle of ceramics and the land from which he took so much stimulus, he is considered as one of the greatest potters who ever lived.

A few years ago in the beautiful Somerset town of Wells, famous for its cathedral, its school and its wonderful period architecture, we held a valuation day inside the cathedral itself, which is also known as the Cathedral Church of St Andrew the Apostle and is the seat of the Bishop of Bath and Wells. A chap called Simon had brought along a most interesting piece, which also came with that little word I keep banging on about,

'provenance'. Simon's aunt had visited the V&A in London in 1982 at a time when Lucie Rie had an exhibition in full swing. Simon's aunt became most enamoured with one of the exhibits, so much so that she decided to write to Lucie and enquire whether it was for sale. Lucie immediately wrote back to say that it wasn't, but that she would be delighted to make a bowl of similar proportions and style.

At that time, London was basking in the spotlight of world attention as the capital of hip, with electropop and the whole New Romantic movement in full swing. The whole world had focused on the city for the wedding of Prince Charles and Princess Diana in 1981, while London's nightclub scene celebrated music and dance with a decadence not seen since Berlin in the 1920s, or the King's Road in the 1960s. Duran Duran, Madness, Adam Ant and Human League saturated the pop charts and overpaid, over-gauche bankers drove red Porsches with whale tails while talking on huge mobile phones. Well, just like London, studio pottery was once again having a resurgence of popularity, especially Lucie's work. Simon's aunt had offered Lucie £100 for her V&A bowl but it seems in the end that she paid £90 for Lucie to make this one-off creation. Hey, that's not bad going! Anyway, it was *Flog It!* time. Will Axon was on form on valuation day, but then suddenly there's Lucie's bowl with her letter to Simon's aunt. Will suddenly went all pessimistic, immediately noticing a crack running from the rim towards the base. 'Did you do that?' came his accusing question. 'No!' said Simon.

Well that was a good start! Will then gave a potted history of Lucie's work and the all-important valuation: yes, it had a wonderful monogram LR stamp impressed on the base; yes, it expressed everything including Lucie's trademark style.

'I'd love a world cruise out of it,' joked Simon. 'Well, maybe we can afford a brochure,' quipped Will sarcastically. No, he went on, it wouldn't make much, but it looked as if Simon might just get Auntie's

Another lovely Lucie Rie bowl, valued at £40,000 to £60,000 by Phillips auction house in London in 2017.

money back plus a tenner. A low reserve with an estimate of £100 to £150.

Just like our valuation, our auction was in Somerset, too, one of my favourite counties. Well, it's not only beautiful and steeped in history, but it's in between my home in Wiltshire and my old stomping ground of Cornwall, so I'm well and truly biased. Claire Rawle was our auctioneer at Tamlyns in Bridgwater and, as the auction got under way, my thoughts were that Will had undercooked the pudding – he'd been a bit mean. Maybe that's harsh, maybe I should say cautious. I was standing there thinking, 'This can't be right. Sure, it's got a crack in it, but this is Lucie Rie! This is provenance. This is lovely.' Guess what! Straight in at £200. Simon was starting to appreciate studio pottery more and more. Then £300 and more, and, when the hammer went down, *crash*! Simon's lovely piece of social history went for £420 plus 15 per cent commission and VAT. Simon was walking away a very happy man.

However, if that was in a gallery today, with the note of provenance, I don't think you'd get much change out of £1,200. Remember, this was five years ago and,

in today's market, £1,200 is about entry level for a Lucie Rie. Given the provenance and the likely restoration, I would guess upwards of £2,000 in the right sale.

More studio pottery came back to haunt Will a couple of years later, this time on the Isle of Wight. It was a small collection of pieces from the Bernard Leach Pottery and, yes, you heard me right: it was Will again. I was thinking, 'What's he going to say this time?' The collection belonged to Alex – five pieces from the Leach Pottery near St Ives. Alex bought them in charity shops and paid 40p for a Leach Pottery spill vase, which in itself should enthuse any would-be collectors and dealers to trawl the charity shops, junk shops, boot fairs and jumble sales! The most expensive piece Alex had bought had cost £30–£40 and Will thought they had all kept the money spent, adding that they were Leach family pottery, not actually by Bernard, but what was he going to say? 'We'll put a reserve of £100, with a £150–£200 estimate.' So there we were, off to Island Auctioneers in Shanklin, with Alex's five pieces, all with impressed maker's marks. Bidding started cautiously at £70. Then, before we knew it, £140, £140, £140 – *sold!* Well never mind, Alex got a £40 profit and enough to invest in some Poole Pottery. But what a steal! It's not all champagne and roses, but there are still bargains to be had. Remember that Alex had paid 40p in a charity shop for one piece. So there you go – that could have been you.

And Will? Well, Will was absolutely spot on. He has a huge amount of experience and as a dad, like me, he's good at calming things down and thinking rationally. None of our experts get it right all the time, but mostly they do. Will's one of our most popular valuers and, having studied to become a chartered surveyor, he looks at things methodically. Learn from this! He's right and he's echoing what I've told you earlier: condition is all. Except when a piece has extraordinary provenance and some history that puts it right up there with the best. And what of Alex? Alex was happy because her lot sold and I have little doubt she'll be scouring Shanklin and Ventnor as we speak for another bargain. So what is my tip? Keep looking and do a bit of homework. To become appreciated studio pottery fully, it's useful to read up on Japanese ceramics. Whether it's work by a lesser-known studio potter such as Clive Brooker, whose Japanese influence is clear and whose work is starting to become appreciated, or you want to collect Bernard's work or his associated family pottery, just keep looking, keep learning and, most of all, enjoy what you do. Clive started making pots in 1956 and his work sold well in Japan, where he had a contract with a department store to supply his take on Ikebana vases. He also went through a blue and turquoise period inspired by the sea in the Caribbean. He lived in the semi-detached suburbia of York Avenue in Stanmore, where his pottery wheel turned out some incredible examples of studio pottery. Yes, Cornwall is the epicentre of studio pottery but what I'm saying is that there is work out there lying unappreciated or unrecognised in garages and on mantle shelves just waiting for someone to come along and go, 'Wow!' When that happens, the work of a previously underappreciated potter will suddenly catch the public's imagination and prices will rise.

Meet the Experts: Anita Manning

'I am an auctioneer and valuer and owner of the Great Western Auctions Ltd in Glasgow.

For as long as I can remember I have always been passionate about antiques, art and auctions, although my career path as a young woman was far from this environment. It was only by chance I got the opportunity in the 1980s to become a buyer for an antiques dealer and learn the trade.

'I had always been fascinated by objects which were beautiful, or told a story. My dad would take me to the Crown Salerooms in Sauchiehall Street in Glasgow as a girl and I suppose it's there that my passion for antiques began. Everything about the auctions fascinated me – the drama, the characters and, of course, the beautiful objects. Great Western Auctions was established by my daughter, Lala, and myself in 1989 and since that time has grown to become one of Scotland's leading independent auction houses.

'I certainly didn't start my life aiming to be an auctioneer – in fact, sometimes I still wonder what I am going to be when I grow up – but I feel that fate put opportunities in my path and, being an adventurous sort of woman, I had a go. I am glad I did because I have one of the most interesting and wonderful jobs in the world. I joined the wonderful *Flog It!* team as

an on-screen expert more than fifteen years ago. Since that time I have also enjoyed appearing on *Bargain Hunt, Flog It!, Trade Secrets, Antiques Road Trip, Cash in the Attic, For What It's Worth, Finding Scotland's Real Heroes, Scottish Passport,* STV's *The Hour* and *Holiday of My Lifetime* with Len Goodman.

'Appearing in antiques programmes allows me to share my love of antiques and art with the public and hopefully to inspire our audience to share my enthusiasm for these beautiful objects. The beauty in craftsmanship and design, coupled with the social history of the objects that I am privileged to see on a daily basis, has been a continual source of joy. The drama and excitement of the auction world has been a most stimulating environment and one that I relish being part of.

'Every auction sale is a new adventure for me. I love the research that can be involved in the process of cataloguing, the crowds and excitement on the day of the sale and the pleasure of standing on the rostrum and hopefully making my vendors happy with the prices their items achieve. There is also the thrill of anticipation, and the auction can be full of surprises, because, until the hammer falls, the outcome is unknown. The auction provides items from the past which have stood the test of time in craftsmanship and design and there is always something to fit every taste.

'The oriental market is especially vibrant at the moment and throws up many surprises. Recently, a badly cracked oriental blue and white vase was consigned to sale and reached a whopping £40,000 against an estimate of £600 to £800. Our vendor and his wife were present in the room and it was wonderful to give them such a terrific surprise. Even though something is damaged it is always better to have it checked.

'I have always welcomed private buyers and collectors to my auction, and encouraged them to experience the theatre of the auction, to become part of the cast. The members of my staff are always happy to give advice to new buyers and everyone is made welcome to our Saturday Sales.

'To be part of the world of antiques has been one of the most satisfying aspects of my life.'

Meet the Experts: Mark Stacey

'As a child, history was my favourite subject at school and I got the collecting bug young: stamps, coins and even phone cards. I clearly remember that my grandparents' house was full of Walsh china, a wash jug and bowl in every bedroom! When I was older, I started collecting small silver, virtue and objects, and started dealing at the tender age of twenty-two. Back then, I collected blue and white transfer-printed ware, eventually amassing a collection of over three hundred pieces and becoming the secretary of the Friends of Blue, a group dedicated to transfer ware!

'After ten years of dealing at fairs and having my own shop, I joined Bonhams as a regional valuer in Hove, then moved to Sotheby's. I learnt so much in my thirteen years at both auction houses from my colleagues.

'I filmed my first programme for *Flog It!* fifteen years ago and have loved the experience, particularly meeting so many people.

'I've been dealing again for the last eight years – the thrill of the chase and the enjoyment of the challenge never goes. I love all periods – and especially one-off or quirky items. For the past four years, I've been focusing on London fairs and broadening my knowledge of mid-twentieth century. That's proved a challenge, too.

'I'm often asked what I collect now and as a dealer, I collect what I can't sell!

'Although I am trying to cope with online in the twenty-first century, an ever-more important marketplace, nothing beats traditional antique dealing and actually touching the objects.'

THE GRAND TOUR

During the nineteenth and early twentieth centuries, Britain's enterprising exploration of the globe transformed itself into the age of empire with travellers, traders and military men bringing home curiosities from the furthest reaches of the globe, and most globes and maps showing a great many countries coloured pink to identify the vast swathes of land controlled by the British Empire. Colonialism took ordinary people from Britain, whether soldiers, missionaries, civil servants or merchants, to some of the most exotic locations on the planet. When confronted with the extraordinary artefacts of the cultures in which they were suddenly immersed, they started to collect ethnographic items that found their way back to Britain as curios, presents for loved ones and, eventually, into the antique shops, auctions and jumble sales where we can find them today.

Prior to the age of empire and the age of steam, however, the only private individuals who left home to go travelling for the sake of it were Britain's wealthy upper class elite. During the seventeenth and eighteenth centuries, long distance travel was neither comfortable nor safe,

with poor communication, storms at sea, bandits, pirates and wars making voyages to far-flung places an experience only for the truly adventurous. Yet it was during this period that the first 'tourists' sallied forth from Britain. You've no doubt heard the well-known saying 'travel broadens the mind' and, while the British aristocracy of the seventeenth century may not have invented the phrase, they certainly took it to heart. When a young nobleman came of age at twenty-one, his education was not deemed complete until he had travelled through Europe to see with his own eyes the continent's architectural marvels and great works of art. Only then could he hold his head up and partake with confidence in polite conversations in the salons of the town houses and country piles of high society back home.

Although some young ladies did embark on the Grand Tour, it was predominantly a male exercise and they could be gone for anything from a few months to more than three years. This really was an indulgence of the super-rich as huge costs would be incurred. A guide travelled with the Grand Tourist to ensure that he saw

Venice and St Mark's Basilica was also an essential entry on the bucket list.

and experienced everything that he was expected to, and some even took servants or a personal chef with them, travelling with an entire entourage. Although the Tourist might meander across Europe for a while, essential places to visit were Paris, where he might learn to fence, ride, dance and speak French, the language of the European elite; Basel or Geneva in Switzerland; and Venice, Florence and Rome in Italy. Few ventured as far as Greece, where there were generally problems with the Turks and local conflicts throughout Europe could also

cause untold delays. The Napoleonic Wars at the beginning of the nineteenth century put an end to the Grand Tour for a while, but once things had calmed down, the Tourists hit the road, and the waterways, once again. When rail networks began opening up all over Europe in the middle of the nineteenth century, making travel far quicker and more affordable for far more people, the concept of the Grand Tour became outdated and it faded away.

What the Grand Tour did most successfully was to spark the aristocracy's interest in collecting, with some investing in an entire new wing or a new building to house their Grand Tour souvenirs, ultimately creating museums to display their collections to the public. Augustus Henry Lane-Fox Pitt Rivers, a nineteenth century army officer, amassed a collection that formed the basis of the Pitt Rivers Museum in Oxford, and the volume of items that Britain's wealthy elite brought home helped to create world-renowned museums and institutions that would eventually attract thousands of visitors every year.

An appreciation amongst the British aristocracy for the talents of European craftsmen may have come partly as a result of the Grand Tour, or may even have provided inspiration for the adventure as there was an influx of persecuted minorities into Britain during the sixteenth and seventeenth centuries. Protestants, vilified in Europe, were eager to find refuge in Britain where, since the reign of Henry VIII, we had had a mixed relationship with Catholicism. Harsh measures, such as punitive taxes and, in the case of Jews, being forced to convert to Christianity, were suffered by the immigrants as the price for safe haven. Yet for all the oppression these people were escaping and the draconian measures

imposed on them, they brought a tapestry of trades with them that nurtured design and introduced fashions that enriched their adopted country.

Here I would like to introduce sculptor and wood carver Grinling Gibbons. Born in 1648 in Rotterdam, the son of an English merchant, Gibbons moved to England around 1667 and I would like to use the words of politician and historian Horace Walpole to describe his talent. He wrote of Gibbons: 'There is no instance of a man before Gibbons who gave wood the loose and airy lightness of flowers, and chained together the various productions of the elements with the free disorder natural to each species.' Gibbons' work was extraordinary and his talent was soon in demand. He went on to work at Windsor Castle, Petworth House, Hampton Court and St Paul's Cathedral.

His carvings on bookcases at the Wren Library, Trinity College, Cambridge, are remarkable, extraordinary even by today's, yesterday's and Greek, Roman and Moorish standards. He was simply a one-off. Diarist John Evelyn saw him working by candlelight through an open window and word soon spread, with Sir Christopher Wren pivotal in recommending that the aristocracy embraced his talents.

A stunning detail from a Grinling Gibbons wood carving at Hampton Court Palace.

The point is that incredible artistry of immigrants (even though Gibbons was actually English and may have completed part of his training in York) simply created more and more interest in Europe in the neoclassical, the baroque and the whole banquet of culture we are so fortunate to have on our doorstep.

European craftsmen brought with them the influences of their native countries, new-to-Britain materials and new techniques, creating a new style for which the educated upper class became voraciously hungry. The interpretation was the craftsman's or the architect's, but they all asked the same question of their clients, 'What do you want?' The answer was invariably influenced by the client's experiences on the Grand Tour and thus the interpretation was undertaken by European craftsmen producing work that reflected the wonders of Venice or of Rome. This is how the genius of Georgian creativity evolved. I adore it.

One can only imagine the wonder with which the children of the British aristocracy

Rome's Sant'Agata dei Goti.

Michelangelo's feat of perspective in painting the Sistine Chapel lying on his back on scaffolding is unparalleled.

took in the neoclassical sites of Europe, although we know that the young tourists indulged in everything that was available to them, including copious amounts of alcohol and the local women. They were, in fact, encouraged to sow their wild oats as far away from home as possible to save their families any embarrassment. One young gentleman, Sir Francis Dashwood, was known to be a particularly rowdy tourist. He also toured more extensively than most of his contemporaries, visiting Russia, Turkey and Syria as well as the more usual places on a Grand Tour itinerary.

When I filmed at West Wycombe House with Sir Edward Dashwood he described the fun and frolics his ancestor, Sir Francis, indulged in during his time abroad (well actually, during his whole life) but specifically the mischief he got up to in Rome. Most notorious were his Good Friday antics of cracking a whip above the heads of Catholics at prayer in the Sistine Chapel. He had earlier seen them submit to mild scourging from the priest and their mimicry of the pain of Jesus on the cross, pretending to beat themselves, had caused Sir Francis to fall about laughing. It wasn't all high jinks and merrymaking, though, as he also had a keen eye, collecting wonderful works of art that were shipped back to West Wycombe. Later, Dashwood had the Italian artist Borgnis paint the wonderful frescos in West Wycombe House. If you couldn't have the original, then a copy would have to do. As I mentioned in the chapter on Pietra Dura, West Wycombe Park is well worth a visit and open seasonally, with guided tours of the house. The grounds are peppered with temples and follies in which you can clearly see the influence of the sites and ruins that Dashwood had seen overseas.

Speaking of Pietra Dura, in 1740 banker Henry Hoare brought home to Stourhead a formidable Grand Tour souvenir in the shape of the Sixtus Cabinet. It's known as the 'Pope's Cabinet' as it was made in Rome for Pope Sixtus V between 1585 and 1590. Hoare bought it from a convent where the last descendant of Pope Sixtus V had been a nun – so we can assume fairly good provenance! The cabinet was designed to look like an ornate Roman church and the Pierta Dura is supplemented with jewels and gilt bronze figures. In 2006-07 it underwent a £50,000 restoration which suggests the huge value it would have were it ever to come up for sale, which is hugely unlikely as it's owned by the National Trust. I can imagine the trembling hand of the assistant housekeepers dusting this amazing piece, fearful of knocking bits off!

I filmed at Stourhead in 2007 with my producer, Andrew, who managed to knock one of our sound recordist Adam's booms into a chandelier in the salon, resulting in a slight flurry of dust and our National Trust chaperone Delia mentioning *Only Fools and Horses*. No damage was done, but you get the drift! Imagine looking after such precious objects on a daily basis as custodian. Some things deserve to be in an accessible and publicly owned collection and the 'Pope's Cabinet' is one such item. We were quickly ushered away for tea and biscuits and, while we all had a laugh about it, in reality you can see why some antiques really should be on national display and in the care of competent custodians who have been schooled in the care of our national treasures! Not far from Mere in Wiltshire, Stourhead and its treasures, as well as the wonderful grounds, are owned by the National Trust, so you can drop by to take a look at the 'Pope's Cabinet', too. Just don't mention the chandelier!

The Grand Tour brought with it, as we have seen, a quest for souvenirs from Flemish tapestries, furniture, fabrics, paintings, neoclassical statuary and columns as well as smaller items like marble obelisks and models of temples. There are country estates today where Grand Tour statues, often dating back to ancient Greece and Rome, sit resplendent at the tops of staircases and in courtyards and hallways – decorations that are often worth, in the current market, more than the properties in which they reside! A number of notable portraits exist, painted by the celebrated artist Pompeo Batoni who lived in Rome. He would position his subjects amongst opulent Italian landscapes and scenery, temples and classical ruins. Although he also painted popes, emperors and dukes, Batoni is believed to have painted more than two

We narrowly avoided a calamity while filming at Stourhead House.

hundred portraits of clients doing their Grand Tour.

I know that society sometimes looks at the great collections of art and sculpture as things 'plundered' from abroad by our privileged upper class, but many souvenir pieces were made specifically for the Grand Tourists of Britain, northern Europe and also North and South America, who travelled the pilgrimage of culture route mostly using daddy's money – and, boy, did daddy often have a lot of

Micromosaic on a nineteenth-century table.

that! Certainly artists like Batoni, who practically made a career out of painting the Grand Tourists, would not have been complaining about being exploited.

Another Grand Tourist, Charles Wyndham, 2nd Earl of Egremont, had his treasures shipped home to Petworth House in West Sussex. Built in the seventeenth century, Petworth House is still home to the Wyndham family, although much of the art collection now belongs to the National Trust, with the house open to the public. Petworth recently starred as a location for Mike Leigh's *Mr Turner* starring Timothy Spall. By the way, *Mr Turner* really is worth a look for the art directing alone and the jewel in the crown is Petworth House. It truly is a wonderful place to visit and it doesn't only boast a Capability Brown-landscaped garden and 700-acre grounds, but also an extraordinary array of artefacts sourced from the Grand Tour. The 2nd Earl had a gallery built just to house his Grand Tour collection. Aside from the largest collection of Turner's art outside any gallery, not to mention the finest Grinling Gibbons carvings, Petworth House is full of sculpture. It's like being transported to the V&A, you forget where you are. Specimen marble-topped tables mix with classical figures of Greek gods,

leaving the casual observer in no doubt as to why John Constable referred to this as 'the house of art.'

If I was starting a Grand Tour Collection I would probably kick off with nineteenth century Sorrento ware with its gorgeously muted tones of olive wood and inlay. You can pick up a piece from as little as a few pounds and you'll find them in antique shops and auction rooms the length and breadth of the British Isles. There are lots of examples available if you look at online auctions, too. In fact, although it is just out of period, I do remember a fine Sorrento ware chess set selling on *Flog It!* It had been valued at £60–£100 but when it went under the hammer at Hansons Auctions, it made a very agreeable £2,200 plus buyer's premium! Our experts don't often get it wrong, but on the day the auctioneer had phone bids coming in from all over Europe. Genuinely, who would have thought that? For our owner, it was another case of smiles all round and real sense of 'Back of the net!'

Marble obelisks and temples are out there too, often made of alabaster and sometimes bronze or indeed a mixture of all three. They make from a few hundred pounds to well into the thousands depending on the maker and the quality of the cast.

Micro-mosaics were also popular, making up everything from jewellery to works of art, mirroring the Roman mosaics and utilising rich vibrant colours for bracelets and earrings, necklaces and rings. Intricately designed and beautifully executed, these are worth investing in as prices are currently on the up.

Now, who remembers the 1970s predilection for cork wall tiles? What about dry flowers displayed on a piece of cork, or a holiday let where the bathroom floor is varnished cork? So how much would you pay for a temple made of cork? We'll find out shortly. Let me set the scene but before I do, let me also suggest you and go and visit the Sir John Soane Museum in London. It

This cork model of the Arch of Constantine in Rome was made by Augusto Rosa in the sixteenth century.

offers such an exceptional opportunity to view items that are a) wonderful, and b) might just turn up in provincial sale rooms, shops or in boot fairs! If you're keen-eyed enough there's always a bargain to be had. Sir John Soane was the son of a humble bricklayer who rose to become professor of architecture at the Royal Academy. His father's inspiration, and that of his elder brother, ushered John into a world of design, taking his inspiration from the classical forms of Greek and Roman architecture. It's here our story starts, because in one of the rooms you can visit, John displayed the most wonderful collection of model buildings. Soan, as he was christened, or Soane as he became, had been fortunate enough to undertake the Grand Tour, absorbing the sights of the ruins of antiquity and running up huge debts in the process. The experience would change his life forever.

I'll talk more about John later, but for now, let's get back to me setting that scene. Having seen a wonderful model temple on display at the Soane Museum, one came up for sale in Hampstead Auctions in London. Let's consider what this model is made of again – cork, which comes from the cork oak, a tree found throughout the Mediterranean, including North Africa and south western Europe, as well as, of course, Italy. Every nine years the cork is harvested and used in lots of ways, such as covering Grandma's bathroom walls and plugging wine bottles. As a side note, I should add that it wasn't until the seventeenth century that this natural and very durable material was used to plug wine bottles. Prior to that oily rags were used, which might well have tainted your Chardonnay a bit.

I'm sure the artist who built the model used cork because it was cheap, easy to work with and also lacked the weight of marble, thus adding to the saleability as it made the transportation of models a whole lot easier. Looking at the model in question, it's attributed to the Naples maker Dominic Padiglione and was made around 1820. Most of the cork models came from either Rome or Naples, which from 1748 onwards became an essential stop-off for Grand Tourists to visit the nearby excavated ruins of Pompeii. Padiglione became supremely sought after for his wonderfully crafted models and back home in London, Soane put together quite a collection of similar pieces. Somehow the model in question had survived and this rare curiosity was about to go under the hammer in a London auction room. What made it all the more interesting was its provenance; it had belonged to the decedent of a tailor who had made clothes for the royal family in Naples. They were wonderfully named the House of Savoy.

The guide price? £5,000 to £8,000. Considering that a similar lot had been auctioned near Stanstead a few months earlier, realising £25,000, it seemed – well, at least in the world of Grand Tour collectors and dealers – a bargain if it made the top end estimate! Consider again that this is made of cork, not mahogany or some precious gem, but it's a Padiglione piece and that's bound to attract a lot more interest! You can almost imagine the auctioneer saying, 'I can start you in the room at …' as bidding got under way.

This was a rather lovely and quite large copy of The Temple of Zeus at Paestum, the original of which is one of the best-preserved Roman temples in the world. Some of you may be wondering why an Italian temple, where Zeus was known as Jupiter, is named the temple of Zeus? Well, it was built by Greek colonists in around 600BC. Italy, of course, was later conquered by the Romans. I'm sure you're also wondering at this point why anyone would amass a collection like Soane? Well, these models weren't just curios, they were used educationally to explain the great classical temples and ruins of the ancient world to architecture students. That helps to explain why so many stately homes and furniture designs of the late seventeenth, eighteenth and nineteenth centuries exude classical form.

With six phone lines furiously bidding, the successful bid went to West Midland furniture dealers, Thomas Coulborn and Sons Ltd. of Sutton Coldfield. Including buyer's premium, they paid £51,700. I believe the Temple is for sale on the Thomas Coulborn and Sons Ltd. website at the point of writing this book.

Let me take you back to the Soane Museum, because collections like this really will educate you in the sort of things you should look out for. I'm not saying you should go out and recreate a Grand Tour collection, although with Intaglios (small plaster souvenir reliefs, often framed) you can start a collection of Grand Tour Roman Emperors or Roman gods for as little as £4 each. When you get enough together, say a small collection of ten or twelve, they'll look stunning framed, maybe using a piece of velvet as a back mount and a boot sale nineteenth century gilt mirror.

With budget airlines offering flights

One of Canaletto's masterful renderings of Venice.

to Venice at well under £100, there hasn't been a better time to get your Grand Tour mojo in gear and sample the delights that attracted the elite of Europe all those years ago. You don't have to be Georgian nobility and with sites like Airbnb you really can do this on a budget. If you get the opportunity, please, please do. I don't think the inspiration factor has lessened since Soane went there, and you'll start to appreciate the intricacies of classical style through the same visual stimulus that incited the passions of architects such as the Adam brothers and Soane, and artists such as Joshua Reynolds.

If you do get the opportunity to visit Venice, take some postcards or download some images onto your phone of artists such as Canaletto. It will add to the romance of your trip and fill you with the sense of perspective and a sensuality that these artists expressed so well. I'm sure that, like me, you'll be looking around and suddenly go 'Wow!' Lost for words – yes, even I am sometimes!

FOLK ART AND VERNACULAR FURNITURE

Well, I'm guessing most of you know what folk art is. If you watch *Flog It!* it should be a fairly familiar subject, but I'll refresh your memory. Folk art covers a multitude of items lovingly made by an amateur or out-of-context hand and the value is in the colour, the hue, the style and the sculptural beauty. As well as practical items such as bowls or utensils, folk art can include something made by the loving hands of a parent of meagre means, perhaps a model castle or a doll, a carved animal or a wagon, once played with and then discarded into the back of the cupboard, only to be rediscovered as a wonderfully aged and coloured antique.

Vernacular furniture has the same sort of attraction as folk art. When we talk about vernacular furniture we might mean, for example, a piece of furniture made in Wales by a country hand. Vernacular furniture is sometimes also referred to as country furniture, meaning that, most probably having been made in a rural area rather than in a big city, it appears more in provincial auctions than in city auctions. Collectors of folk art may also collect vernacular furniture as the two sit very well together. There are, of course, particularly wonderful pieces of folk art and vernacular furniture that feature in auctions held by the great salesrooms such as Sotheby's and Christie's.

Top London dealer Robert Young says on his website (www.robertyoungantiques. com) that folk art and vernacular furniture have enjoyed a renaissance because, 'Critics, curators and collectors variously claim this is due to its fundamental unpretentious integrity, that its bold graphics and limited palette have been a source of inspiration to some twentieth-century artists and that its raw, untutored style is a refreshing escape from contemporary concepts and ideologies.' This genre of furniture holds a special place in my heart.

Before I talk about this subject I want to talk about me – no, don't go and put the kettle on just yet, I mean in the sense of me as a dealer and what makes a good dealer. In understanding that, we will delve into folk art and vernacular furniture. I also want to introduce you to the primitive stick chair, slipware pottery, rush lights, polychrome trade figures and love tokens.

I spent several years trading out of my shop in Kingsbury Street in Malborough, Wiltshire, living upstairs and developing a number of clients, some of whom became lifelong friends. In the words of Peter Blake, a collection is a form of conceptual art and I endeavoured to present my stock as a kind of collection, in a setting that relaxed and inspired customers and, hopefully, the visual stimuli would enthuse them enough to buy something. I specialised in vernacular furniture and, although I sold period furniture and occasional twentieth-century pieces, I predominantly went for vernacular sculptural pieces that would fit well in any country home.

To start vernacular off, let's look at stick-back chairs. If you are not familiar with them, then have a look at these photos. These chairs were made all over the United Kingdom, predominantly in places such as High Wycombe and Staffordshire, becoming the basis of chairs produced for the mass market that many of us probably remember from school.

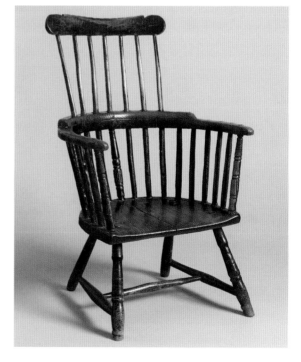

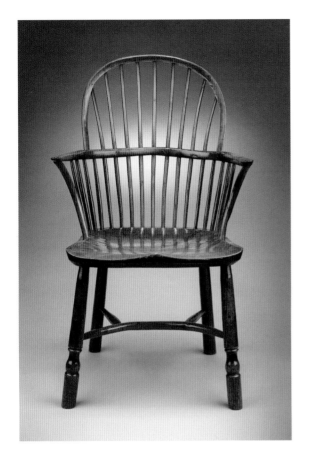

I firmly believe that one of the best investments in the world of art and antiques is the primitive stick-back chair. The one-off chair represents great value for money. They're underappreciated, tactile documents of our regional social history. Part of our heritage, without a doubt.

If you know what to look for, it will be the best investment you'll ever make. Not only will it outlast you, but your children as well, for as little as £300 to £400. It's great fun searching the dealers' stock and salerooms to put together a harlequin set of six to eight stick-backs. Different heights, sizes, woods and hues. It's a slow process searching, but with every trip out you can glean a little more knowledge from the specialist dealers and eventually that odd few you have found become a carefully curated sculptural display.

It's comical watching family members and friends discreetly finding their favourites. Comfort invariably wins over style, and before long a whole game of musical chairs ensues throughout the dinner party or even at breakfast time, with some people reluctant to get up, for fear of the next person's seat-hopping. I've seen it all and heard it all, with 'that was my chair', 'I was sitting in that' or 'It's my turn now'. It's a great way of bringing history alive. I've even used smaller ones as bedside tables, and the odd one in the bathroom with folded white towels for the Shaker look. As a dealer, I always had several in stock and they were a real joy to sell.

My favourite is the West Country Comb Back, with a three-part arm, popular from the eighteenth century onwards. This has three separate sections of arm, cut and shaped with the centre section lap-jointed over the outer sections to create the frame for the sticks to pass through, as opposed to the earlier, single 'steam-bent arm'. The three-part arm offers a more robust durability. I love the primitive stake leg construction, which has always been associated with the most elementary furniture, used by the poor and especially the rural labouring classes. This chair has stood the test of time. It looks great today, and its crudeness has a sculptural quality in the contemporary interior. A large, generous seat and well-placed tapering sticks, holding the back cresting rail with some form of outline decoration, are a must-have for me. The chair must also have a wonderful colour and surface – evidence of an interesting life.

From the seventeenth century onwards, regional craftsmen produced these wares for the middle and labouring classes as practical, functional pieces of furniture. By the eighteenth century, the stick-back was affectionately known as the 'Windsor Chair'. It's got nothing to do with Windsor or royalty, it's just that there were various centres mass producing them by hand, throughout Buckinghamshire, High Wycombe and Slough, with easy access to plenty of elm, beech, and ash growing in the chalky soil of the Southern Chilterns.

So the term 'Windsor Chair' is now used to describe any regional stick-back chair, be it made in the Thames Valley, the Northeast, the West Country or wherever. It describes a chair whose legs and back are socketed into a solid seat by virtue of a series of holes drilled right through it. Then the legs, backstay and spindles (all hand-drawn) are driven into the seat, and secured by a wedge in the way that an axe handle is fixed to the head. The chair is made and assembled while the wood is in the 'green', freshly felled, unseasoned timber, as it is so much easier to work, given that the craftsmen were using relatively low-powered pole lathes, treadle lathes, adzes and chisels. Once the chair has been assembled, the moisture content will start to dry out and, as it does so, the grain will tighten, shrinking the socket holes and making the joint rock solid.

Wherever there was a fresh supply of newly felled, green timber, there would be a bunch of healthy blokes in a well-organised team, each with a specialist job: 'bodgers' set up their pole lathes to do the turned parts; seats were fashioned out with a hand adze (tractor-seat style) by the 'bottomer'; steam-bent parts were prepared by the 'bender'; and all sawn parts were cut out by the 'benchman'.

The final assembly was carried out by the 'framer'. This was a small factory system of itinerant craftsmen, labouring in 'pop-up' workshops that could appear at a moment's notice almost anywhere.

Elm is the usual timber for seat boards as the grain never runs straight. It's ambiguous and interlocking, does not split easily under pressure and is available in broad widths. Ash is commonly used for legs and struts since it cleaves easily into poles and can be bent to shape by steaming. It is tough and resilient.

There are many variations, such as the steam-bent bow or hoop back, and the comb back, all differing in shape and size. Some have turned decoration on the legs and stretchers. Paint finishes most commonly used were blue, green, red or yellow. There are also two forms of hoop used: one that was cleft into a lath shape and the other round in section, made from saplings and sprung into shape. There are an almost infinite variety of permutations. The great thing about the stick-back is that it is invariably made from locally sourced timbers and it will have a regional identity.

Now, I mentioned Robert Young earlier and he is certainly one of my favourite dealers. I filmed with him a few years ago and I've often revisited his showroom in Battersea, just across the Thames from the throng of antiques shops in Chelsea's Kings Road. He has a host of celebrity clients and art students regularly visit his exhibitions. He also travels abroad to the US every year, selling, among other things, the ever-popular stick-back chair, one of the mainstays of antique collecting. Robert was taking time out from an exhibition when I visited him to find out what he had to say about vernacular furniture, and he had readied three items to look at.

It's the individuality and personality of vernacular pieces that attract Robert – their charm, their history, their texture and their line. They also have a sculptural quality and that all combines to make something special, something out of the ordinary, and that's where their commercial appeal lies.

Robert started by juggling a very nice and slightly classical joint stool/table that was made of oak with, as he said, 'no veneer or superfluous bits and bobs'; it had something about it that made it more than an average piece, and it had presence. Although naïve, the piece had a thin top, which is so much more complicated for a joiner or carpenter to create than a chunky top. It's more demanding of the maker and more elegant in the finished piece. Where it overhung, the top gave an exquisite line. Colour is all important and I look for a finish that's like a wet conker – colours drawn from woodland inspiration, like a forest in autumn. The colour gives evidence of its age, whether the piece is big or small.

Robert also showed me a lambing chair that I suggested looked thrown together, and he agreed. It could have been made by a coffin maker who worked with broad planks. The value was in the surface and by that Robert meant the wear and the digs and knocks. The chair would have been in a tavern and there was a niche underneath to sit a lamb! How sweet is that?! The shepherd would bring an orphaned lamb into the tavern in the evening and have some ale and feed the lamb by bottle. I volunteered that you were buying into the history but for Robert it was all about the sculpture of the piece. He pointed out initials and dates scratched in, too. Can you imagine that on a Chippendale sideboard? No, of course not! That's where the two styles differ. Classical is all about condition and originality while folk art is all about the piece having been lived in, its use marking its age. Robert is highly critical of items

that have been tampered with, believing that originality is all. He pointed out some beading that you would barely notice as having been replaced, but to Robert's utter credit he highlighted it, admitting it *had* been replaced and that it detracted from the appeal of the piece.

Then came a weird-looking, out-of-proportion chair that I just loved and, as I was about to find out, was far more primitive than at first glance. One arm was higher than the other, and the back rails were out of line. Whoever made it had no drawings to work from. Maybe it was made by a tradesman with a vision. Maybe he made it as a gift. We'll never know – it's simply a one-off. Timber on this sort of furniture is always immaculately chosen and always regional. The maker couldn't afford to import or buy fancy timber, so he simply used the best that was available.

This chair was used in a home where life took place by the fire, which was the centre of the home. No glue was used; it was entirely pegged and pinned, small metal nails pushed into the pegs to ram them into place. The chair had traces of red paint, which Robert explained had been to protect it from the elements because in summer it may well have gone outside. Another school of thought suggested the red was used to emulate the look of mahogany. Almost certainly it was for protection. Slowly, Robert's description turned the chair from just a seat into a warm and embellished story where, for just a moment, I felt transported back in time. Robert taught me what to look for and that's so important.

So do you get it? Folk art is something made by an amateur hand using available materials to create something to be loved and used. Then, through the centuries, it takes on a sculptural beauty and, whether a piece of furniture or a picture or an item made to be used, it becomes a piece of art in its own right.

Tips on what to look out for? Always look for good colour and patination. Signs of wear: rub marks from weary hands on the chair arms; worn feet and undulating stretchers; darker tones and grease where hair touches the back and crest rail; darkening in areas where the chair has been picked up by dirty, hardworking hands; and wear and decay on the legs at floor level. Look for real signs that the chair has had a useful life. This will be the document of its history.

It's not just about the maker but the user as well. Rustic, functional repairs add personality and are endearing if they are old enough to be part of the chair's history. Later 'restoration', as Robert pointed out, is to be avoided. Large, shaped-out seats without excessive wear and strong arms that still have some spring are what to look for, and consider whether it is a practical sitting height. Traces of original paint that have gone crusty are a gem. Welcoming lines: good overall shape, high back, minimum turnings, preferably without a centre-back splat.

Never buy a chair that has been stripped, or bleached, recoloured with dyes and waxes, or had the legs built up to put the height back on worn legs. A clever restorer will always make the join on a ball or ring turning. If the legs are turned, check the grain in the wood runs the same, with the right spacing and figuring. Restoration or repairs in this area will also be newer wood, recoloured darker to blend in with the existing in order to deceive. Stay away! If the chair was low, leave it low. It takes on a different use. If you combine some of these rules you will have a great investment. Prices start around £300 for mid-nineteenth century to £700 for mid-eighteenth century. Having one of these in the house will always put a smile on your face when you look at it, and give you more inspiration to be creative.

Places to buy include David Swanson Antiques, Petworth, Sussex; Robert Young Folk Art, Battersea, London (both dealers always have great examples in stock). For further reading try *Oak Furniture: The British Tradition* by Victor Chinnery; *The English Regional Chair* by Bernard D. Cotton.

Rush nips are another, ever-popular example of folk art and you can expect to pay up to a few hundred pounds for an exceptional tabletop one. Rush nips? What am I on about? OK, some of you may remember your grandparents using them as they had a bit of a revival during the Second World War and . . . hold on . . . what are they? Rush nips are crudely made metal stands for burning rushes and dried straw dipped in tallow. They are lamps – well, a very rustic and immensely charming lamp – and incredibly ingenious, although admittedly a bit of a fire hazard. The actual nips, as they are known, are very sculptural pieces. They are made of metal, which will have oxidised and browned over the years to give a wonderful patina of age. The nip holds a rush core, simply the middle of a rush that has been harvested during summer and autumn, then dipped in tallow once peeled and dried. Any handy kitchen fat was used, which would no doubt kick

off a storm of nanny-state lectures about carcinogens if people were doing that sort of thing nowadays. They first appear in literature in the seventeenth century but have probably been around for far longer. An average rush would burn for only fifteen minutes or so and, while it has a candle-like flame, it also gives off a lot of smoke, not to mention a pong! Sometimes rush nips are mounted on a block of wood, sometimes they are three-cornered and simply sit on

An iron nip.

three legs. There are also tall versions like standard lamps and even wall-mounted versions. Imagine having to swap them over every fifteen minutes, though!

The standard-lamp nips are on a larger turned base, or a crude forged-iron one, some with a half-metre-tall toothed shaft to ratchet the nip up and down to adjust the height of the light. This type of floor light was often used as a task light, by carvers, knitters and other home craftsmen and craftswomen. Today they make good money as they are so, so sculptural. The zigzag ratchet shaft looks a bit like a saw blade and it's quite ingenious, really, although adjusting the height looks as though it's more of an event than a practicality. Nips look great on their own or holding a dried, long-stem flower. And, if anyone questions your choice, tell them oil prices will soon be so high that we'll all be going back to the seventeenth century!

Robert Young sold a wonderful example of a table or mantle nip not so long ago. It was on a carved-pyramid wooden base, painted a wonderful dark brown. Attached was an angular, almost art-deco-looking, candleholder with a drip pan attached. I can almost imagine it used on special occasions when visitors came over on Sunday afternoons – then, it would be back

to rushes for a smoky week! On this one, the candleholder was on the counterweight, the counterweight acting as a pinch mechanism to hold the nip tightly as it burned. More primitive versions would lack the drip pan where the candleholder is fashioned.

Polychrome figures are always sought after by interior furnishers for their animated appearance, the colours washed out with age and the gesso crackled and worn in places where the tactile nature of the piece has drawn attention from a thousand hands that have all left their marks. Often advertising pieces or for ecclesiastical use, they have somehow weathered the centuries and made their way into the trade as much-loved and very commercial furnishing pieces. Religious figures of saints may come in parcel gilt and can be great to animate a room or even bring a bit of fun and mischief to an environment.

In the nineteenth century, gnomes became popular and brought a whole new fascination that kept resurfacing decade after decade. With the advent of plastic, gnomes took over the gardens of suburbia and every clichéd bungalow garden had at least a couple of gnome tenants up to around 1980, when they were considered vulgar and banished to the back of the garden shed. A few die-hard gnomes hung on, making the news when sailors stole them to take on world tours, sending postcards and photos home from far-off places – very wrong but hysterical all the same.

Now the time has surely come for a renaissance, certainly of folk-art gnomes. I love them! Every home should have a gnome! Many were made in Germany – indeed there's a whole area of gnome manufacture where terracotta was used. Yes, pottery gnomes from around the turn of the nineteenth century to the twentieth are much sought after.

The first gnomes were made in Thuringia in Germany and one of the grandfathers of gnome making was Philipp

Griebel. A trained porcelain maker, he opened a factory making moulds for animals but soon added gnomes, which became a huge hit not only in Germany, but England and France, too. The oldest gnome in Britain is in Northamptonshire at Lamport Hall where *Flog It!* filmed a couple of seasons ago. As a self-confessed gnome lover, I was so excited to meet such an elder statesman of gnomedom! The 10th Baronet, Sir Charles Isham, first introduced gnomes to Lamport Hall in the 1840s and is credited with starting the craze that swept Britain. He'd inherited the hall aged twenty-six, loved gardens and clearly loved the fun and the quirky too, populating his rockery with a colony of gnomes from Nuremberg.

As an alternative to gnomes, invest in religious figures, gnarled with age and possibly missing bits and pieces here and there. They are often gilt and sometimes polychrome, which simply means multicoloured, and they turn up in salerooms all over the place. They look great on a shelf or recumbent on a dresser or against a wall. As every auctioneer will tell you, they always make good money which means they always make a great investment.

Now slipware pottery will, I'm sure

you agree, seem a bit like the great-aunt of studio pottery, and in some ways it is. So what's it doing here? Well, it goes so wonderfully with folk art and vernacular furniture, whether a trio of old jugs on top of a court cupboard or a crisscross-patterned bowl full of fruit on a side table, the colours just peeking through. If you Google slipware, it will say, 'Slip is an aqueous suspension of a clay body, which is

using slip to create different patterns and textures. Some pieces are so prized that they have made their way into art museums and collections the world over.

Sgraffito might sound like a new kind of street art, but it was used in a process where the maker scratched through the colours to create a pattern, giving a surface texture a bit like an ice-cream cornet. It was kind of mass-produced on a studio pottery

Although it looks like it might have been made just a few weeks ago, this sgraffito plate is from Iran and dates back to the tenth century.

a mixture of clays and other minerals such as quartz, feldspar and mica.' Why can't they embellish it with a few well-chosen adjectives such as 'evocative', 'quirky' and 'beautiful'? The effects were manifold, with amateur hands and well-known potters

scale for the rural classes, who embraced its functionality without perhaps realising how it would one day become a collectable antique. Combing and dragging developed as styles of artistry from different potters, some using sticks and small, handmade implements, predominantly working in brown, yellow, cream and black, all of which had a high lead content. Yellow had an especially high chromatic hue, which simply means it was a solid block colour.

Colours and hues were strong and there's nothing wishy-washy about eighteenth-century and early-nineteenth-century slipware. Today they are sought after by collectors and interior designers – even twentieth-century pieces that look very similar make good money. You'll know an honest piece by the thickness of the glaze and the weight of the vessel. Some edges were left rough, some rolled and some even thumb-pinched. Bowls, jugs, plates, the whole gamut, were treated to crosshatched patterns and combing. Harvest jugs make an absolute fortune, as we will see in a moment.

Regionally, the main makers of slipware were in Staffordshire and Ewenny in Wales but other provincial areas had their own styles too, such as Verwood in Dorset. A glazed earthenware harvest jug in a wonderful globular form was sold at Christie's for £11,875 in 2010. It was a well-documented piece made in 1797 by potter Thomas Bartlett, in Bideford, North Devon. Thomas decorated it with foliage and an image of Ceres, goddess of the harvest, using a sgraffito technique. Pieces like this, if you are ever lucky enough to own one, will fit in with any

An earthernware glaze mug of Lord Rodney, made c.1782.

interior, I promise you. Colour, condition and decoration are all.

Around London, jugs with faces were popular, often with an old man pulling his beard or wringing his hands. We're fortunate enough to have some stunning examples dating back to the fourteenth century on display in museums and heritage centres, and this style is known as anthropomorphic. What does anthropomorphic mean? It simply means making or adding human form to something not human, so, by making the jug in the form of an old man, it becomes anthropomorphic.

Like Bernard Leach, slipware potters would use any old brushwood or wood shavings swept up from the floor to fire their kilns, and they would throw stuff at the pots while they were firing. They might open the kiln at a very high temperature, throwing a handful of copper dust at the pots, creating the wonderful colours we see today.

Of course, potters copied or emulated styles and, just as neoclassical designs became popular with the aristocracy and merchant classes, makers of slipwarecopied styles they had seen. Perhaps they worked on a country estate and had heard about some newfangled designs, not even having seen them at all, or perhaps someone had sketched something or, indeed, something from the local dump had caught their eye. Slipware, therefore, was more about interpretation than exact design, whereas classical pottery was all about symmetrical form and likeness of pieces. Slipware, by its nature, is organic and one can imagine the makers using sticks and broken implements to scratch and work patterns, experimenting with glazes and slips as much as with powders and ores, copper and sand. Remember when looking

This large plate (or charger) was prominently signed by Thomas Toft almost 350 years ago, the signature looking much like a modern brand logo.

at examples to buy that the best examples are festooned with names and poetical text and, most importantly, they are dated and initialled by the maker.

One potter who embraced organic and classical styles was Thomas Toft. Thomas was based in Staffordshire in the seventeenth century and, while the coarse earthenware clay he used worked wonderfully with the black and green slips and the lead-oxide glaze, it was his intricate decoration that made his pottery stand out. His work, if ever it comes up, creates a real buzz in the trade, in auction houses and online. These were special pieces, truly unique one-off items, no two ever exactly the same.

A whirligig made in the 1920s.

By now you know all about my love of vernacular furniture and primitive oak and hedgerow-wood chairs. Well, what better ornament for a court cupboard than to line up three big, bold, primitive-slipware jugs along the top – maybe offset with a rush nip and a whirligig on the opposite corner? I'm sure we all remember whirligigs from shops such as Woolworth's or bought at the seaside when we were kids, but they're not just novelty toys. There is a whole fraternity of collectors specialising in eighteenth- and nineteenth-century wooden pieces. Again, Robert Young is an aficionado and it's worth checking his website to learn a bit more. Whirligigs are huge fun and give a bit of animated sculpture to an interior. They are often in the form of windmills and soldiers and sometimes animals, faeries or young ladies pumping, and, the harder the wind blows and the faster the sails turn, the faster they pump away. The sight of a soldier and young lady pumping together gives an open window a wonderfully comical air.

Weathervanes also fall within the world of folk art, often cut out by a local blacksmith or maybe made of board. Prices range from a few pounds to many thousands, yet, for a few hundred pounds, a well-weathered and oxidised silhouette of a fox on a moonlit night will give huge amounts of amusement for generations to come. It can also create a wonderful ornamental addition to a dresser or a console table or niche.

Willow work is sometimes overlooked but it is definitely another must-have item for any country cottage, perhaps to display fruit in the kitchen or cut flowers in the sitting room. Use willow practically and, if nothing else about it inspires you, I am sure you'll find it an antidote to cracked plastic and Tupperware any day of the week. The weight of a trug or basket is often determined by the type of fruit it's been made for, but, if you become as absorbed by the wonderful weave as I am and – yes, I'm going to say it again – the sculptural beauty of a piece, then look at the vast range of associated items made of willow, too. There are willow chairs and tables and, although condition remains all-important, there are examples available from a few pounds in a local auction to many thousands of pounds for a very rare and unusual lot.

Makers were everywhere, but there were enclaves of creativity such as the Somerset Levels, so look into the styles and makers. Log baskets are usable, desks and chairs great for cottages and conservatories, and, if you're into your classic cars, what better way to spend an afternoon than to take a drive with an old wicker picnic basket in the boot and sit in the grounds of a National Trust property soaking up the sun?

Somerset is the real home of willow and its use in basket-making goes back generations. Picturesque villages with romantic names such as North Curry and Stoke St Gregory were full of 'withy beds', supporting the whole industry surrounding

The stunning, haunting sculpture, The Willow Man.

willow. Willow was also used to bind barrels and its strength and durability made it a sought-after commodity. If you're collecting English willow, do be aware of the Chinese willow and French willow, which can often be mistaken for English willow. There's nothing wrong with either French or Chinese willow, but, if you are being type-specific, then eventually, as you become more absorbed and more familiar with it, you'll note the different colours and textures that the weavers have used.

While filming in Somerset I was fortunate enough to meet the sculptress of the *Willow Man*. I'm sure many of you remember the wonderfully dark, classic suspense movie *The Wicker Man*, which was set off the coast of Scotland on Summerisle, an idyllic community almost lost in time, governed by Lord Summerisle, wonderfully played by Christopher Lee. Lord Summerisle's grandfather had brought paganism back to the island and the community as a whole had adopted a devil-may-care attitude to life while growing and exporting their apple crop. When the harvest failed, the islanders decided they needed a human sacrifice. Enter Edward Woodward as Sergeant Howie from the mainland. I won't spoil the plot, but it's incredibly well filmed, with

some wonderful music and an unexpected twist at the end. In the film, overlooking the sea, we see a huge wicker man soaked in tallow, the cage in which the sacrifice will be burned alive. That might sound like poetic licence for the sake of a good movie, but the Roman historian Tacitus described human sacrifices by the Druids using this method some two thousand years ago. I'm told that, until very recently, the feet of the massive Wicker Man film prop still existed on location in Scotland, which, considering the film was released in 1973, is pretty good going.

So, when *Flog It!* asked me to go to Somerset, mentioning *The Wicker Man*, I felt a little uneasy! I was in the car on the way there thinking, 'Summerisle? Somerset? Wicker Man? Invite? Ignite?' But I had nothing to fear! I'd gone along to meet willow artist Serena de la Hay, a very talented lady. Born in Africa, she then spent time in Australia, from where many of her influences clearly came. She has spent twenty-five years living in Somerset and uses local materials to create her wonderful abstract forms, which take their inspiration from the landscape around her. She also lectures in rural crafts and environmental art.

I went along to meet Serena and to visit

an exhibition of her work near Glastonbury, out on the Somerset Levels. You may know of her as she was commissioned in 2000 to undertake the construction of *Willow Man* that we all see when we drive north along the M5, just near Bridgwater, where it's on the western side of the motorway. It has become well known as *The Withy Man* or *The Angel of the South* in homage to Antony Gormley's *Angel of the North*. Serena was commissioned by South West Art to create something for the millennium and her wonderful sculpture was unveiled in September 2000 to huge acclaim. Sadly, the first version was burnt down by mindless idiots a few months later, but the sculpture was rebuilt by Serena in 2001, this time with a moat around it. In 2006 *Willow Man* even received a haircut!

I also met up with Nigel Hector, whose family own and run English Hurdle at Curload near Stoke St Gregory, based in their ancient farmhouse, where Serena also has her studio. Save the odd flood, it must be the most stunning of places to work every day. Nigel and the craftsmen who work at English Hurdle not only farm willow, but produce all manner of baskets, ornaments, furniture and fencing using natural willow. They are also involved in planting willow to prevent riverbank erosion. It's due to people such as Nigel that our rural crafts are kept alive, and they really do matter, because, once a craft dies out, it's lost for ever.

I remember meeting an upholsterer called Bernie a few years ago and he traced his heritage back to Stourhead, where his ancestors learned their trade working with Chippendale Junior. Imagine that, a direct connection. Imagine, too, the tricks of the trade and the techniques that are handed down from one generation to another, then – whoosh – they are gone. If I could impose CITES (Convention on International Trade in Endangered Species – see Chapters 6 and 7) on these trades and crafts I would. Even if you have no empathy with the past, you must realise that, by revisiting the past, we secure the future. The world is ever changing and environmental disasters are forever in the news, so what better way to manage our planet than by using its natural and renewable resources in an intelligent and empathetic way? That and, of course, realising the value of antiques as one of the oldest forms of recycling!

Whatever your interest, do consider the social and sculptural, and, yes, elemental beauty of folk art. It really is one of my favourite areas of antiques collecting.

Admittedly, I'm no fan of painted furniture in general terms, but, if that's your bag, do make sure you're not buying three coats of trade emulsion buffed with furniture wax. In my mind there's just too much painted furniture around. Yes, it has its place but it's become almost like a reaction to the pine-stripping excesses of the 1980s that banished so much wonderfully combed and distressed nineteenth-century decoration. Ensure you buy from a respected and trusted dealer who knows about the items, and read, read, read about your interest. Honestly, education is all. Just because something is old, it doesn't follow that it's valuable. I'm not writing to dictate taste either. That is as personal as what colour socks you like or your favourite pudding. So buy what you like. Yes, that's what I keep banging on about: buy only what you like! That way you might have a few regrets but the basis of your collection will become your work of inspirational art. Always remember, however, that, if you have put a small collection together and you're a bit tired of it, why not sell it? That way you can keep trading up. We've sold some unusual things on *Flog It!* in the past and I often wonder who's bought some of the pieces we've sent to auction. Has a vase been converted to a lamp base, or has a

Love spoons were carved not only as love tokens but also to demonstrate a young man's skill and, therefore, his ability to make a decent living.

piece of social history ended up back in someone's cupboard?

What you'll notice about folk art and vernacular furniture dealers and collectors is the way they display things, often within their own space, which, as I often say, gives a piece importance. It's a hard task to make a busy environment of pieces work but, if you manage it and if you can pull the effect off, then it can look absolutely stunning.

I'm going to end with a word to inspire: love. Well, in fact, love tokens, which primarily come in the form of spoons. I was fortunate enough to make one on the show, which I was allowed to keep and which became a present to my wife. I incorporated my initials into it and those of Charlotte. It's only something small but it means a lot to us both. People have been falling in love since forever but, as a traditional woodworking craft, the making of love spoons dates back to the seventeenth century. The oldest known love spoons in Britain are in St Fagans National Museum of History near Cardiff, the tradition having flourished in Wales, although there are slightly older examples in Germany, as love spoons were also carved in Eastern Europe and Scandinavia. Presenting a beautifully carved love spoon to his intended wasn't just a token of his affection, but also showed the young lady's father that his daughter's suitor had acquired a skill and would probably, therefore, be able to find work in order to look after his daughter. Love spoons could be incredibly intricate and some, given as wedding presents at one time in Norway, were even linked by a wooden chain, the idea being that the husband and wife would eat together using the spoons to symbolise their being joined by marriage. The two spoons, and the links of the chain, would all be carved from the same piece of wood. Imagine the skill and patience that would have to go into that!

So, love tokens are lovingly made, and made with love in mind, making them highly collectible and creating a great way to inspire a love of antiques! Whatever you choose to collect, I hope that you will have picked up some useful tips in this book, but don't stop reading now – go straight out and carry on researching. Remember, there is no substitute for knowledge and knowing what you are looking at is by far and away the best way to enjoy it most. That, after all, is what collecting antiques is all about: enjoying the history, enjoying the beauty and enjoying yourself. Have fun!

ACKNOWLEDGEMENTS

A big 'thank you' to my wife, Charlotte, and the family for putting up with me and giving me so much support.

Thanks to Becky Faulks and Andrew Blackall for help and inspiration on the book.

And to John Ord for all his fabulous photographs.

For further reading about antique furniture, I highly recommend the books by Adam Bowett, Victor Chinnery and Bernard Cotton.

For more information on style and expertise visit Robert Young and Will Fisher at their galleries, or visit their websites (www.robertyoungantiques.com / www.jamb.co.uk/antique-furniture). They helped me to develop a discerning eye.

Other exciting places to visit for inspiration are Lorfords Antiques in London, David Swanson in Petworth and Spencer Swaffer in Arundel, as well as Drew Pritchard in Conway, North Wales. And, further afield, it is always worth looking for ideas on the website of Obsolete Inc in California (www.obsoleteinc.com).

PICTURE CREDITS

Rex, pages:

2: Geoff Moore/Rex; 9: Granger/REX; 10: REX; 11: Nils Jorgensen/REX; 13: REX; 129: Granger/Rex/Shutterstock; 130/131: REX/Shutterstock; 148, 152: Adam Partridge/Bournemouth News/REX/Shutterstock; 155, 158, 165: Richard Gardner/REX/Shutterstock

Getty, pages:

22: Print Collector/Getty; 24: UniversalImagesGroup/Getty; 40: Peter Macdiarmid/Getty Images; 41: Peter King/Fox Photos/Getty Images; 42: Frank Scherschel/Time & Life Pictures/Getty Images; 49: Bettmann/Contributor/Getty Images; 44: Kurt Hutton/ Stringer/Getty; 65: Hulton Deutsch/Getty; 83: Graham French/BIPs/Getty Images; 128: DeAgostini/Getty; 134, 135: English Heritage/Heritage Images/Getty; 154: Tony Evans/Getty; 163: Wesley/Keystone/Getty

PA Images, pages:

57: Matt Crossick/PA Images

WikiCommons, pages:

3: WikiCommons; 18: Met Museum/WikiCommons; 20: Michael D. Beckwith/WikiCommons; 28: Jorge Barrios/WikiCommons and Sailko/WikiCommons; 29: Rogers Fund/WikiCommons; 37: Rauantiques/WikiCommons; 56: BB/WikiCommons; 62: Enchufla Con Clave/WikiCommons; 67: WikiCommons; 72: WikiCommons; 75: Adam Jones Ph.D/WikiCommons; 76: Wmpearl/WikiCommons; 77: Mackelvie Trust Board/WikiCommons; 78: John Atherton/WikiCommons; 81: Houston Museum of Natural Sciences, Texas/WikiCommons; 93: Auckland War Memorial Museum/WikiCommons; 93: Skagway Museum/Wikicommons; 100: Metropolitan Museum of Art/WikiCommons; 103: Museo Nacional de Artes Decorativas, Madrid, Spain/WikiCommons; 174: Roman Bonnefoy/WikiCommons; 176: Camster 2/WikiCommons; 177: Livioandronico 2013/WikiCommons; 178: Jörg Bittner Unna/WikiCommons; 180: Josep Renalias/WikiCommons; 181: Daderot/WikiCommons; 183: Daderot/

PICTURE CREDITS

WikiCommons; 185: Giovanni Badoer/
WikiCommons; 186: Met Museum/
WikiCommons; 197: Rogers Fund/
WikiCommons (left) and Maryele/
WikiCommons (right); 199: Rogers
Fund/WikiCommons; 200: Daderot/
WikiCommons; 203: Locutus Borg/
WikiCommons

National Trust, pages:

26: National Trust Images/Andreas von
Einsiedel; 33: National Trust Images/
Bill Batten; 110: National Trust Images/
Andreas von Einsiedel

Alamy, pages:

16: Andreas von Einsiedel/Alamy; 17:
William Wilson Photography/Alamy;
27: Andreas von Einsiedel/Alamy; 35:
National Trust Photolibrary/Alamy ;
37: The National Trust Photolibrary/
Alamy Stock Photo; 38: mauritius images
GmbH/Alamy Stock Photo; 45: The
National Trust Photolibrary/Alamy Stock
Photo 47: Fremantle/Alamy Stock Photo;
101: Heritage Image Partnership Ltd/
Alamy Stock Photo; 112: Heritage Image
Partnership Ltd/Alamy Stock Photo; 120
top: jozef sedmak/Alamy Stock Photo; 120
bottom: PRISMA ARCHIVO/Alamy
Stock Photo; 122: age fotostock/Alamy

Stock Photo; 124: Paul Christian Gordon/
Alamy Stock Photo; 125: Neil McAllister/
Alamy Stock Photo;126: Kevin White/
Alamy; 132: Douglas Lander/Alamy; 133:
Heritage Image Partnership Ltd /Alamy;
138: B Christopher/Alamy; 140: ZUMA
Press, Inc./Alamy; 147: age footstock/
Alamy; 173: Bildarchiv Monheim GmbH/
Alamy; 202: David Carton/Alamy;

Bridgeman, pages:

46: National Trust Photographic Library/
Andreas von Einsiedel/Bridgeman 59:
National Army Museum/Bridgeman;
60: Look and Learn/Bridgeman; 61:
Bridgeman, 63: Historic England/
Bridgeman; 70: Mark and Carolyn
Blackburn Collection/Bridgeman; 91:
Brock, Charles Edmund (1870-1938)/
Private Collection/© Look and Learn/
Bridgeman Images; 91: Natural History
Museum, London, UK/Bridgeman
Images; 95: Private Collection/Bridgeman
Images; 106: Lady Lever Art Gallery,
National Museums Liverpool/Bridgeman
Images; Charles II carved and painted
mirror/Private Collection/Bridgeman
Images; 108: Devonshire Collection,
Chatsworth/Reproduced by permission
of Chatsworth Settlement Trustees/
Bridgeman Images; 141 The Sherwin

Collection Leeds, UK/Bridgeman Images;
145: Yoko Honda/ Private Collection/
Bridgeman Images; 150: Musée des
Antiquités Nationales, St Germain-en-
Laye, France/Bridgeman Images and
Fitzwilliam Museum, University of
Cambridge, UK/Bridgeman Images;
156: Peter Kinnear/Bridgeman Images;
160: Werner Forman Archive/Bridgeman
Images; 198: National Maritime Museum/
Bridgeman

British Museum, pages:
68: Trustees of the British Museum; 79:
Trustees of the British Museum

Shutterstock, pages:
66: Shutterstock

The Prince's Foundation, pages:
8, 11, 12, 13

**Courtesy of Robert Young Antiques,
pages:**
188, 189, 194

**Reproduced with permission of Anthea
Morton-Saner on behalf of Churchill
Heritage Ltd, pages:**
43: Churchill Heritage Ltd

Wellcome collection, pages:
89: Science Museum, London; 118:
Wellcome Collection

Any photographs not listed here are by
John Ord of Kinetic Studios, who worked
closely with the author on the photography
for this book.